Fulbright
v.
Americraft Industries
and
Parker

Fifth Edition

Case File
Trial Materials

Fulbright v. Americraft Industries and Parker

Fifth Edition

Case File
Trial Materials

Michael H. Ginsberg
Pittsburgh, Pennsylvania

Based on the case file by

Edward R. Stein
Anthony J. Bocchino
Frank Rothschild

With contributions from

Peggy Flanagan, PhD
Lane Cannon
Claudia Cornelison

NITA®
National Institute for Trial Advocacy

Address inquiries to:

Reprint Permission
National Institute for Trial Advocacy
357 McCaslin Blvd., Suite 200
Louisville, CO 80027

Phone: (800) 225-6482
Email: publications@nita.org

FBA 2192
eFBA 2193

ISBN 979-8-88669-192-4
eISBN 979-8-88669-193-1

ASPEN PUBLISHING

Official co-publisher of NITA.
aspenpublishing.com/NITA

Contents

Expert Materials

Case Synopsis

John Fulbright has sued Jamie Parker and Parker's employer, Americraft Industries, for personal injury damages arising out of a car-motorcycle accident that took place on Fifth Street in Nita City on July 20, YR-2. The plaintiff, Fulbright, claims that the defendant, Parker, negligently operated a Cadillac automobile while engaged in the business of Parker's employer. The defendants have admitted that Parker was acting in the scope of employment, but have denied all other material allegations of the plaintiff's claim and affirmatively allege that the plaintiff was negligent and that the plaintiff's negligence was the sole proximate cause of the accident.

The plaintiff alleges that he suffers from traumatic brain injury as a result of the accident, which will require lifelong treatment, including medication. He further claims that this condition has prevented him from obtaining a college scholarship and has limited his income potential because he cannot become a professional football player. The defendants deny that the plaintiff's traumatic brain injury was caused by this accident.

Some of the photographs in this case file were created using AI. These should be treated as original photographs that can be admitted into evidence based on the testimony of a witness with personal knowledge of the subject matter of the photograph.

INTRODUCTION

If this case is used for a full trial, the following witnesses may be called. In a two witness per side trial, plaintiff should call John Fulbright and either Jordan Anderson or Blake Brown, and defendant should call Jamie Parker and either Alex Markham or Jordan Anderson.

Plaintiff:

John Fulbright
Blake Brown
Tatum Harris
Morgan Myer, PhD

Defendant:

Jamie Parker
Alex Markham
Reagan Flanagan
Lee Tippett, MD

Witnesses that may be called by either party:

Officer Tracy O'Brien
Jordan Anderson

This case file uses the "year minus" format or "YR-_" to denote years. In this format, YR-1 means the current year minus one year, YR-2 means two years ago, etc. Please substitute the actual year when using this case file.

Exhibits are available for download here:

bit.ly/43axcZr
Password: Fulbright5

Stipulations

1) There is no helmet law in the State of Nita.

2) The parties have stipulated that the formula for calculating how many feet per second a vehicle travels is as follows: miles per hour × 1.47 = feet per second.

3) The diagram shown as Exhibit 1 is to scale.

4) The deposition exhibits have been premarked at trial, for identification purposes only, using the same numeric designations. The parties have not stipulated about their admissibility.

5) The signatures on the depositions are authentic, and their authenticity shall not be challenged.

6) This trial has been bifurcated into a liability phase and a damages phase. Advocates shall not present evidence as to the extent of Fulbright's lost earnings and/or medical expenses during the liability phase.

7) Any physical or visual discrepancies between witnesses as described in the case materials and witnesses as portrayed by their "actor" are to be ignored.

8) Parties and witnesses may be portrayed by a person of any gender.

9) Parties and witnesses had the opportunity to review their depositions and make any relevant changes.

10) At trial, Officer Tracy O'Brien will constructively testify to the following:

    I was the police officer who investigated this car-motorcycle collision, but I did not see the incident occur. The motorcyclist, later determined to be John "Jackie" Fulbright, was taken to the hospital by an ambulance. There was some evidence that Jamie Parker, the driver of the car, had consumed alcohol at lunch, but Parker did not seem to be impaired, and I did not notice any signs of intoxication. I allowed Parker to leave the scene so Parker could return to work; Parker did not appear to be injured. I believe that both Fulbright's speed and Parker's failure to ensure that there was a clear lane contributed to the collision. I did not issue either a citation. I provided Fulbright with a statement to sign while he was in the hospital.

11) At trial, Blake Brown will constructively testify to the following:

    I am 40 years old and work downtown in an accounting firm. On July 20, YR-2, I was walking down the Fifth Street sidewalk across from Ray's restaurant, headed towards Forest. When I got to the corner of Forest and Fifth, I saw Jackie Fulbright coming down Fifth street on his motorcycle. He was in the lane closest to my sidewalk and was driving towards me. I recognized him from the helmet he was wearing—I am a huge fan of the Nita City Central Cougars and have seen Jackie play over the past few years. The helmet is made to look like his football helmet, including his number 8. I remember that Jackie waved back at me. He wasn't driving very fast, about normal for that road. Then I saw that Cadillac pull out in front of him. Jackie never had a chance to avoid it. I found Jackie's helmet after the crash and gave it to the policeman so he could return it.

12) At trial, Tatum Harris will constructively testify to the following:

I am currently an assistant football coach at Nita State University. I coached Jackie Fulbright when he played for the Nita City Central Cougars. I have never seen a better high school quarterback anywhere. During one of our practices, after Jackie's accident, I decided to have the team do some full contact drills. The kids needed to get an idea of game-feel so they wouldn't be caught off guard in a real game once the season started. One of our defensive ends hit Jackie from his blind side. He was lying still on the ground for a couple of seconds. I went over to help. He had to move pretty slowly, but he was able to walk off without any extra assistance. He really got his bell rung. I kept Jackie out of the rest of practice, but he seemed back to his old self by the end of it. I know players do get concussions sometimes, so I sent him to the school nurse the next morning to check for a concussion. Jackie never ended up playing his senior year.

13) At trial, Reagan Flanagan will constructively testify to the following:

I am the chief financial officer of Mangez-A-Trois, Inc. Ray's Steakhouse in Nita City is one of our properties. Ray's was located on Fifth Street until the end of YR-1. Back then, Ray's used the E-Serve software system for tracking orders. It was pretty reliable, but it crashed occasionally like any software. Our waitstaff would enter the table number, number of guests, and their orders on a touchscreen monitor, then the system would send the info to the kitchen and the bar. When an order was ready, our waitstaff would be notified by pager, pick up the order, and bring it out to the customers. E-Serve also printed off the checks. In theory, I guess waitstaff could punch in the wrong item by mistake and ask the chef or bartender to make the correct item instead. I provided the records from July 20, YR-2, pursuant to the subpoena I received. Exhibit 23 shows all two-person tables that ordered either a chicken caesar salad or a martini that day.

14) Advocates should inform the court and opposing counsel of any constructive testimony they plan to argue in closing prior to the end of their case in chief. Advocates may do so by directing court and counsel to the relevant stipulation number. If an advocate provides this notice, then both teams may argue, reference, or rebut that constructive testimony in closing as if it had occurred during the trial.

15) Both Plaintiff and Defendant have personal knowledge of Officer O'Brien's police report and may lay the proper foundation to introduce it, subject to hearsay and hearsay within hearsay objections.

16) All witnesses are familiar with Exhibits 10, 11, and 12.

17) Alex Markham is familiar with Exhibit 23, and can testify to the E-Serve system as described in Flanagan's deposition.

18) Witnesses are familiar with the exhibits they reference in their statements and depositions.

IN THE SUPERIOR COURT OF NITA COUNTY
STATE OF NITA

JOHN FULBRIGHT, Plaintiff v. AMERICRAFT INDUSTRIES and JAMIE PARKER, Defendants.	)))))))))	Civil Action No. 23-1234

COMPLAINT

COMES NOW, Plaintiff in the above-styled civil action, and brings this Complaint against the above-named Defendants, and in support hereof, shows the Court as follows:

PARTIES, VENUE, AND JURISDICTION

1. Plaintiff John Fulbright ("Plaintiff") resides in the County of Nita and is subject to the jurisdiction of this court.

2. Defendant Americraft Industries is a for-profit business that may be served with process at its headquarters at 137 Central Roan Street, Nita City, Nita 24601 ("Americraft"). Defendant Jamie Parker ("Parker") may be served with process at Parker's residence located at 4211 Granger Street, Nita City, Nita 57815. Americraft and Parker are referred to collectively as "Defendants."

3. Defendants are subject to the jurisdiction of this Court because they are Nita residents.

4. Venue is proper in this Court because Defendants reside in Nita County and the incident that forms the basis of this action occurred in Nita City, Nita County.

BACKGROUND

5. On July 20, YR-2, Plaintiff and Parker were involved in a car-motorcycle collision (the "collision") that took place on Fifth Street in Nita City.

6. Plaintiff was operating a YR-4 Honda Shadow Aero motorcycle traveling eastbound on Fifth Street, a one-way street with multiple lanes.

7. Parker, operating a YR-3 Cadillac four-door sedan, was leaving the parking spot on the southernmost lane of Fifth Street and traveling eastbound.

8. The collision occurred when Parker recklessly attempted to enter the center lane of traffic on Fifth Street without yielding to Plaintiff.

9. Plaintiff suffered bodily injuries because of the collision.

10. At all relevant times, Plaintiff exercised due care for his own safety.

NEGLIGENCE

11. Parker owed an ordinary duty of care to the motoring public in general, and to Plaintiff in particular, to operate a vehicle in a reasonable and non-negligent manner.

12. The collision was caused by the negligence of Parker.

13. The collision was caused by Parker's reckless driving.

14. The collision was caused by Parker's negligence and recklessness for driving under the influence of alcohol.

15. The collision was caused by Parker's negligence and recklessness for failing to yield to Plaintiff's vehicle.

16. The collision was caused by Parker's negligence for failing to operate a motor vehicle in a safe manner.

17. Plaintiff's injuries were caused by Parker's negligence.

VICARIOUS LIABILITY

18. Plaintiff hereby adopts the allegations in the prior paragraph as if they were expressly asserted herein.

19. At all times relevant to this action, Parker, who was responsible for exercising reasonable care while driving, was employed by Americraft and was acting within the scope of employment with Americraft.

20. Americraft is responsible for Parker's conduct under the doctrines of respondeat superior, agency, and/or apparent agency.

21. As a proximate result of the negligence and recklessness of Americraft's employee, Plaintiff suffered bodily injuries for which Plaintiff is entitled to compensation.

DAMAGES

22. Parker is liable for Plaintiff's injuries and damages sustained, physical pain and suffering, and all other elements of damages allowed under the laws of the State of Nita.

23. As a result of Parker's negligence and recklessness, Plaintiff experienced physical pain and suffering.

24. As a result of Parker's negligence and recklessness, Plaintiff suffered mental anguish.

25. As a proximate result of Parker's negligence and recklessness, Plaintiff suffered denial of social pleasure and enjoyment.

26. As a proximate result of Parker's negligence and recklessness, Plaintiff suffered a loss of earning capacity.

27. Plaintiff seeks to and is entitled to recover for:

    a. Personal injuries;

    b. Past, present, and future pain and suffering;

    c. Mental anguish;

    d. Loss of capacity for the enjoyment of life;

    e. Loss of earning capacity;

WHEREFORE, Plaintiff respectfully requests:

1. Process issue as provided by law;
2. Trial by jury against Defendants;
3. Judgment be awarded to Plaintiff and against Defendants;
4. Plaintiff be awarded damages in amounts to be shown at trial;
5. Plaintiff have such other relief as this Court deems just and appropriate.

Submitted February 25, YR-1.

/s/ Charli Sivan, Esq.
Nita Bar No. 1236789
Attorney for Plaintiff

IN THE SUPERIOR COURT OF NITA COUNTY
STATE OF NITA

JOHN FULBRIGHT, Plaintiff v. AMERICRAFT INDUSTRIES and JAMIE PARKER, Defendants.	)))))))))	Civil Action No. 23-1234

DEFENDANTS' ANSWER TO COMPLAINT

COME NOW, Defendants in the above-styled civil action and bring this Answer to the Plaintiff's complaint, and in support hereof, show the Court as follows:

PARTIES, VENUE, AND JURISDICTION

1. Defendants are without knowledge or information sufficient to admit or deny the allegations in Paragraph 1 and, on that basis, deny the same.
2. Defendants admit the allegations in Paragraph 2.
3. Defendants admit the allegations in Paragraph 3.
4. Defendants admit the allegations in Paragraph 4.

BACKGROUND

5. Defendants admit the allegations in Paragraph 5.
6. Defendants admit the allegations in Paragraph 6.
7. Defendants are without knowledge or information sufficient to admit or deny the allegations in paragraph 7, and on that basis, deny the same.
8. Defendants deny the allegations in Paragraph 8.
9. Defendants deny the allegations in Paragraph 9.
10. Defendants deny the allegations in Paragraph 10.
11. Defendants deny the allegations in Paragraph 11.

NEGLIGENCE

12. Defendants deny the allegations in paragraph 12.

13. Defendants deny the allegations in paragraph 13.

14. Defendants deny the allegations in paragraph 14.

15. Defendants deny the allegations in paragraph 15.

16. Defendants deny the allegations in paragraph 16.

17. Defendants deny the allegations in paragraph 17.

CONTRIBUTORY NEGLIGENCE

18. At the time of the events alleged in the complaint, Plaintiff was behaving negligently by driving too quickly, failing to pay attention to Defendant Parker's vehicle, and failing to properly protect himself from harm by wearing a helmet.

19. Plaintiff's negligence was a proximate cause of Plaintiff's injuries.

VICARIOUS LIABLITY

20. Americraft Industries denies Plaintiff's assertions of vicarious liability as laid out in paragraphs 18–21 of Plaintiff's Complaint.

DAMAGES

21. Defendants, having fully answered the specific allegations set forth in Plaintiff's Complaint, deny that Plaintiff is entitled to any recovery against Defendants as alleged in paragraphs 22–27 of Plaintiff's Complaint.

WHEREFORE, having answered fully, the Defendants pray that the Court dismiss the action against the Defendants with prejudice, with all costs being taxed against Plaintiff.
Submitted March 23, YR-1.

<u>/s/ Troy Montez, Esq.</u>
Nita Bar No. 345678
Attorney for Defendant

Depositions

DEPOSITION OF OFFICER TRACY O'BRIEN

My name is Tracy O'Brien. I am a Nita City police officer. My badge number is 7274. I have been a Nita City police officer for six years. I am a patrol officer. I was the officer who investigated a car-motorcycle accident that took place on Fifth Street on July 20, YR-2.

I looked at the report you showed me and the attached witness statements. Those make up my report of this incident (Exhibits 2–5). To be honest, I do not have much independent recollection of this accident other than what is in my report. I will answer your questions to the extent I can remember.

I was called to the scene of this accident at approximately 2:15 p.m. Just as I arrived, so did an ambulance. A young man, who I later determined to be John Fulbright, was lying unconscious on the pavement on Fifth Street between Clay and Forest streets. I helped the ambulance attendant load Fulbright into the ambulance and was informed that he would be taken to General Hospital.

I then investigated the accident scene. It was fairly easy to determine what had happened. A motorcycle, driven by Fulbright, collided with the front left quarter panel of a Cadillac driven by Jamie Parker as Parker attempted to enter into the center lane of traffic on Fifth Street from the parking space in the southernmost lane of Fifth. As a result of the collision, Fulbright was thrown to his landing place.

I interviewed the witnesses, who originally included Parker, Jordan Anderson, and Alex Markham. I spoke to these three witnesses together. As we were talking, we were approached by Blake Brown. Brown handed me a helmet that Brown reportedly found in the northernmost lane of Fifth Street approximately halfway between the point of collision and where Fulbright came to rest. Exhibit 9 is a photograph taken of the helmet at the police station before returning it to the Fulbright family. I completed my interviews of all the witnesses. I allowed Parker to leave before the others because he had an important business appointment.

I attempted to get witnesses to come to the station the next day to sign statements. Anderson declined. Parker originally agreed, but declined to sign a statement the next day on the advice of counsel. Markham signed a statement the next day. I did not get a signed statement from Brown.

As I recall, there was some evidence that Parker had consumed some alcohol at lunch, but he was not obviously intoxicated. Parker was clear and coherent and exhibited no signs of impaired function.

From everything I could determine, the accident was unavoidable and occurred when Fulbright left the northernmost lane of Fifth Street to pass a truck, and just as Fulbright entered the center lane, he collided with the Parker vehicle that was pulling into that lane of traffic. I am sure that Fulbright's speed had something to do with causing the accident, but so did Parker's failure to ensure that Parker had a clear lane to pull into traffic. Rather than issuing two citations, one for speeding to Fulbright and one to Parker for failure to yield, I decided to issue no citations at all and leave it to the insurance companies to work it out.

I confirmed this version of the accident with Fulbright at General Hospital later that evening. It was the end of a long day when I spoke to him. I typed up the statement when I got back to the station, and I took it out to his house the next day and had him sign it.

You have shown me a diagram of the accident scene on Fifth Street and it is accurate (Exhibit 1). It shows the layout of the area where the accident happened. Exhibits 10, 11, and 12 are photographs that accurately show Fifth Street and the entrance to what was formerly Ray's Steakhouse as it appeared on the date of this accident, the only difference being the name Yank Sing on the building and awning instead of Ray's Steakhouse.

I have given full and complete answers to all of your questions. I will read my deposition for accuracy when it is transcribed.

I have read the foregoing, and it is a true and accurate transcription of my deposition given on January 15, YR-0, in the offices of the plaintiff's attorney.

Tracy O'Brien
Tracy O'Brien

Subscribed and sworn before me this 15th day of January, YR-0.

Harry Gibbons
Harry Gibbons

Notary

Deposition of John Fulbright

My name is John Fulbright, but everyone calls me Jackie. I am nineteen years old and live with my parents and my sister Imogene, who's sixteen, at 2942 Rivington Road in Nita City. My dad is the regional manager for a chain of sporting goods stores, and my mom is a grade school teacher.

I am currently a first-year student in a two-year program at Nita Community College, where I am enrolled in an associate program in science. When I receive my certificate, I hope to continue my education at Penn State, where I intend to major in education. It should take me an additional three years to complete my degree. My long-term goal, now, is to teach science in high school and become a football coach.

I was involved in a car-motorcycle accident on July 20 of YR-2, which was the summer between my junior and senior years of high school at Nita Central High School. While in high school, I was the quarterback on my school's football team in my sophomore and junior years. I started both years and was named second team All-State in my junior year. I had received over twenty letters from colleges expressing interest in recruiting me for their football programs. Exhibits 13–16 are four of those letters. I had also been elected the captain of my team for my senior year. My dad was an All-American linebacker at Penn State and had played for three years for the Detroit Lions before he hurt his knee and had to retire. It was my goal to attend Penn State on a football scholarship and hopefully be good enough to make it in the pros. Penn State was one of the schools that sent me recruiting information. Although Penn State was my first choice, I was also interested in Michigan, Colorado, and Texas. I may have set my sights high, but I had been told by my coaches that those schools were well within my range. As it turned out, I never found out because of this accident.

The accident happened on July 20 of YR-2 at about 2:00 p.m. I had the afternoon off from the summer camp I worked at for kids with muscular dystrophy. My older brother Bobby had muscular dystrophy. He died when he was twenty-two years old, in YR-6. I began to work at the camp the summer after he died. Anyhow, I made plans to have lunch and then spend the afternoon with my girlfriend at the time, Riley Howard. I was supposed to pick her up at 1:30. Riley and I had been going together since we were in junior high. She was a swimmer on our swim team. We broke up the fall of my senior year. Our relationship had always centered around sports and being active, and after what happened to me, our relationship changed, and we eventually went our separate ways.

The accident happened, as I said, around 2:00 p.m. I was driving east on Fifth Street on my Honda Shadow Aero, which was my motorcycle at the time. Fifth is a one-way street going east. It has three traffic lanes, but one of them (the southernmost lane) is used primarily for parking—except at rush hour, when all three lanes are in use. I had been following a semi-truck in the far left-hand lane for several blocks before I decided to pull out to pass him. The truck was traveling really slowly, about twenty miles per hour, and the fumes were bothering me. I checked the center lane for traffic behind me in my rearview mirror and pulled around the truck. I had just passed the intersection of Forest and Fifth when I pulled out to pass. I had traveled about fifty to seventy-five yards in the center lane when this Cadillac that had been parked in front of Ray's Steakhouse pulled out suddenly in front of me. I didn't have a chance to even swerve, and I ran into the front left side of the Cadillac and went flying through the air. The next thing I remember, I woke up in the hospital.

My motorcycle was totaled in the wreck. I had bought it in June of YR-3, right after I got my driver's license, with some money that my grandfather left to me in his will. I bought it used from someone on Craigslist. It had about 8,000 miles on it. Exhibit 17 is the photo I sent to my grandmother to show her my new cycle. I rode the bike whenever I could. In the winter, I either took the bus or borrowed my parents' car. I would say that I was an experienced motorcycle rider—or at least as experienced as you can get in a year or so.

I've been told that I didn't have my helmet on when I landed after being hit by the car and that they found my helmet on Fifth Street, just up the street from Ray's Steakhouse. I know I had the helmet on as I was riding down Fifth Street. It was a hot day, and to tell the truth, I would have preferred not to have had it on, but my parents had grounded me the summer before (YR-3) for not wearing my helmet, so I always wore it. The only thing I can guess is that it flew off when I got hit by the car. Because of the heat, I might not have had the chin strap buckled. Yes, that's my helmet in that picture (Exhibit 9).

I've also been told by the police that the driver of the Cadillac said that I was going about fifty miles per hour at the time of the accident. That's just not true.

Q: How fast were you going when you first saw the Cadillac pull out from its parking space?

A: I couldn't have been going more than thirty-five; probably thirty to thirty-five.

Q: What was the speed limit on Fifth Street in that area?

A: I'm not sure, but I think it's either twenty-five or thirty.

Q: Then you were speeding just before the accident?

A: I wouldn't say I was speeding. Traffic generally moves along Fifth Street at thirty to thirty-five miles per hour, and that's what I was doing.

Fifth Street is a shopping/restaurant area with stores, offices, and restaurants. There are also some office buildings in the area. The diagram you showed me looks accurate as to what's located in that area (Exhibit 1). Ray's Steakhouse was located between Forest and Clay on Fifth, on the south side of Fifth. I ate there a couple of times with my parents. It had valet parking for its customers as well as a parking lot out back of the restaurant. There is also parking on Fifth Street in front of the restaurant that's used by people eating at the restaurant as well as people shopping at the stores near there. As I said, I've traveled on Fifth a lot. It's not unusual for people to pull out from the parking spaces on the south side of the street or from the parking lot for Ray's. When you ride a motorcycle, you have to be especially careful about people pulling away from curbside parking because they don't seem to notice motorcycles, even though I always rode with my headlight on to make myself more visible.

I've been told that I was unconscious for about a half-hour from the time of the accident until the time I woke up in General Hospital. I had a real bad headache and a lot of scrapes and bruises, but luckily I didn't have any broken bones. I must have used my football instincts to protect myself when I hit the ground. They kept me in the hospital for a few hours for observation. I was told by the doctor that they were concerned about a concussion, even though the x-rays they took did not show any skull fractures.

That evening, in the hospital, I was visited by a police officer who was investigating the accident. He was the one who told me that driver of the Cadillac said I was going fifty miles per hour. I don't know how Parker could say that. First off, I wasn't going that fast. Second, if Parker saw me, why did Parker pull out in front of me? The cop asked me a lot of other questions, including why I wasn't wearing my helmet. I told him that I was, just like I told you today. I also told him about getting grounded by my parents for not wearing the helmet in the past. I remember that he told me to take it easy, that he wasn't going to give me a ticket.

Anyhow, the police officer wrote up a "statement" for me to sign. It obviously wasn't everything I said to him, but I had a really bad headache and couldn't really concentrate on reading so I just signed it and gave it back to him. Looking at what you just showed me (Exhibit 5), that looks like my signature. It's basically right about what happened and what I told him, but it's not in my words, and as I said, the police officer didn't write down everything I said. He just took some notes, and the next day he brought me this paper to sign. The doctor had also given me some pain medication. I don't know whether that kept me from telling the officer what happened.

Q: How were you after the accident?

A: I was sore for a few days, and I had a pretty bad headache for a day or two.

Q: Any other problems from the accident?

A: I've had recurring nightmares about the accident, headaches, lightheadedness, ringing in the ears, and occasional blurred vision.

Q: By the time football practice started, did you think you had recovered from the accident?

A: Yeah, by the time practice started I felt pretty good.

On September 12, the week before our first game, I stood up and almost passed out. I was dizzy and confused. I felt weak, and had some numbness in my arms and legs.

I went to my doctor to be checked out and she sent me for some scans. She told me that she was checking me over to try to figure out what caused the numbness and dizziness. My first question was whether I would be able to play in the opening football game. I didn't even consider what turned out to be true—that I'd never be able to play football again.

Yes, there was something relatively unusual that happened on that day. Usually, no one was allowed to hit the quarterback in practice, but that day we were having full-contact drills, and Billy Parrish, our 250-pound defensive end, blindsided me after I threw a pass. I never saw him coming, and he hit me pretty hard and rung my bell. What I mean by that is that for a couple of seconds I didn't know where I was and I felt a little woozy. Coach had me sit out the rest of practice, just to be sure I didn't have a concussion, but I really didn't think much of getting hit at the time. I played quarterback for the seven years I was involved in organized football, and getting your bell rung is just a hazard of playing football. It didn't happen to me often, maybe three or four times, but as I said, it's not really a serious injury.

As to other injuries in football, I had gotten a lot of bumps and bruises, but I never missed a game due to injury. The only time I missed a game was in my junior year when I was suspended for a week of school because I got caught cheating on a quiz in my chemistry class. I was allowed to stay on the team because it was the first and only time I had ever done anything like that and because I took a make-up quiz that I passed. So I only missed one game.

The symptoms I experienced that day continued over the next several weeks and kept me from ever playing another down of football. I was also prevented, until recently, from driving a car—the doctor had to report the dizzy spell to the state motor vehicle department and they revoked my license. Last month I was allowed to start driving a car again because Dr. Barron was convinced that it was safe as long as I stayed well rested and was not dizzy when I was starting to drive. I'm not allowed to engage in any contact sports or any activity where it's likely I can hit my head. For example, I'm not allowed to ride a motorcycle or go water skiing. Dr. Barron, who has been my only doctor since I was a kid, set these limits, and I've done what she told me to do.

I wasn't the best student in high school. I guess I put too much emphasis on football, but it was my first love. My GPA was about 2.4. I had taken the SATs, and my score was just under 1100. I remember I was pleased because I easily made the requirements to be a scholarship athlete in college. My dad used the scores to yell at me for not applying myself in my studies.

Although I missed the football season in my senior year, I still graduated on time from high school. Because of my condition, I needed to stay near home, and because of my grades, I was only able to get into Nita Community College. I've done pretty well there as a science major. My grade point average is 3.6. As I said, I hope to get into Penn State when I graduate with my associate degree in June. Given my father's connection with the university (he is an active alum), I have been told informally that if my grades continue at their current level, getting accepted should not be a problem.

I guess I'll always wonder how my life would have been without this injury, but I don't think I can dwell on that. I've tried to make the most of my life since then, but I still get the urge to get out on the field every time fall comes around and that can be depressing. Like my father says, at least I never got my knees banged up, so I won't be hobbling around when I get to be his age.

Yes, Exhibit 24 is my profile on JockDates.com. That's a dating site for athletes. Yes, I described myself as "fit." I certainly wasn't going to say that I suffer from traumatic brain injury. How many matches do you think I would have gotten if I did that? Yes, I've had a bunch of matches, and sometimes they led to a relationship, including the one I'm in right now. She's a tennis player at Nita State. I told her about my TBI after our first couple of dates. I always did that when I was interested in a girl. Three or four times, suddenly the girl didn't seem interested in me anymore. Other times, it didn't seem to matter to them. No, it didn't matter to Olivia, my current girlfriend.

Yes, that's me in Exhibit 24 playing flag football. I play it whenever I can since it's the closest I can come to real football. I also play basketball, volleyball, golf, tennis, and extreme Frisbee. And I'm a really good ping pong player.

I have given full and complete answers to all your questions. If I remember anything else, I'll let my lawyer know so that he can inform you.

I have read the foregoing, and it is a true and accurate transcription of my deposition given on January 12, YR-0, in the offices of defendant's counsel.

John Fulbright
John Fulbright

Subscribed and sworn before me this 12th day of January, YR-0.

Harry Gibbons
Harry Gibbons

Notary

Deposition of Blake Brown

My name is Blake Brown. I am forty years old and live at 410 Eighth Avenue in Nita City. I am not married and don't have any roommates. I am employed in downtown Nita in an accounting firm. I am a graduate of Nita Central High School and am a longtime fan of the Nita Central football team.

On July 20, YR-2, I saw the wreck where John Fulbright got hurt. Jackie was the star quarterback on the Nita Central High School football team before he got creamed in this accident by that guy in the Cadillac. I was a big fan of his.

On the day that Jackie got hurt, I was walking on the sidewalk of Fifth Street on the side across from Ray's restaurant. I was headed toward Forest. When I got to the corner of Forest and Fifth, I saw a motorcycle coming toward me on Fifth in the lane closest to the sidewalk I was on. The diagram you showed me looks like what Fifth Street looks like where the accident happened (Exhibit 1).

I had stopped to make sure it was safe to cross Forest when I saw the motorcycle. As it got closer, I could see the motorcycle rider was wearing a helmet that looked like a football helmet—it had the number 8 on it. I then realized that the guy on the bike was Jackie Fulbright, so I waved to him. He waved back and then pulled into the center lane of Fifth to go around a big truck that was a little bit ahead of him.

I watched as he rode down the road, when this Cadillac just suddenly pulled out in front of him from being parked on the south side of Fifth in front of Ray's Steakhouse. Jackie never had a chance to get out of the way even though he wasn't going very fast, and he ran right into the side of the Cadillac and went flying through the air. I couldn't tell how fast Jackie was going in miles per hour, but it wasn't very fast, about normal for that road. The next thing I knew, he was lying real still in the road. I ran up to see what happened, but I really couldn't see much. I called 911 on my cell phone and tried to help, but there were already a bunch of people standing around Jackie and I felt like I was in the way. Pretty soon a policeman and an ambulance came, and they took Jackie away. As I started to walk away, I saw Jackie's helmet on the side of the road. It was near the curb on the north side of Fifth, about halfway between where the driver of the Cadilac hit Jackie and where Jackie landed. It must have gotten knocked off when he hit the car.

I picked up the helmet and made my way across the street to where the policeman was. The helmet was scraped. I gave it to the police officer so he could give it to Jackie. I told the police officer what I witnessed. Exhibit 9 shows Jackie's helmet that I picked up from the street after the accident.

The next thing I heard about this accident was when a man who said he was with the insurance company for the Cadillac came to see me at my house. He told me that he had gotten my name from the police and asked if he could talk to me and get a written statement from me. I told him everything I told you. He tried to get me to say that I wasn't sure about whether Jackie had on his helmet, but I told him, like I told you, that it was the helmet that made me recognize the guy on the bike as Jackie. When I wouldn't change what I told him, he left without ever letting me sign a statement.

I have also talked to you and Jackie's lawyer about what happened, when you came to my house to talk to me.

I have told you everything I can remember about what happened.

I have read the foregoing, and it is a true and accurate transcription of my deposition given on January 18, YR-0, in the offices of the defendant's lawyer.

Blake Brown

Blake Brown

Subscribed and sworn before me this 18th day of January, YR-0.

Harry Gibbons

Harry Gibbons

Notary

DEPOSITION OF JAMIE PARKER

My name is Jamie Parker, and I live at 4211 Granger in Nita City. I am forty-one years old and work as a sales manager for Americraft Industries, a manufacturer of diversified heavy industrial equipment. I'm married. My spouse, Avery, and I have three children—Zayden, who is sixteen; Mira, who is thirteen; and Violet, who is eight.

I have been with Americraft ever since I graduated from the University of Nita in YR-20 with a degree in business administration. I started with the company as a salesperson and have worked my way up the ladder to where I am now, the head of a national sales force that numbers twenty people. My job is to manage and supervise the sales staff. I also service some of our best accounts in the State of Nita and surrounding states.

One of our best customers is the Abbott Aluminum Company in Nita City. They manufacture all manner of aluminum products from storm doors and windows to some automobile parts. They are an active company, always looking to open up new markets, and when they venture into the manufacture of a new product, they have, over the past fifteen years, come to us for the design and manufacture of the machinery necessary to implement their growth. The president of Abbott Aluminum is David Slater. He is a very busy man, and it is difficult to get in to see him, so I mostly work with Jordan Anderson, Mr. Slater's employee who is responsible for purchasing materials for Abbott.

As a sales person, it is important to cultivate relationships with buyers. You obviously can't sell anything if you don't get to speak with the potential customer. As a result, I take the time to cultivate good relationships with these people. One of the ways I show my appreciation is by taking them out to lunch or dinner. That way they know I appreciate their assistance and, hopefully, will continue to be helpful in getting me access to their bosses.

On July 20 of YR-2, the day of the accident we're here to talk about today, I took Jordan Anderson to lunch at Ray's Steakhouse in Nita City. I had been in to see Dave Slater that morning, and so I asked Jordan if I could take them to lunch. I can't say that this was the first time I had asked Jordan to lunch or dinner, but it was the first time that they accepted. As I've said, such invitations are part of my business.

I met Jordan at Ray's Steakhouse, which is located on the south side of Fifth Street between Clay and Forest streets, at approximately 12:30 p.m. Fifth Street is a three-lane, one-way, eastbound road. The southernmost lane, in front of Ray's, is used for parking, except during rush hour, when all three lanes are available for traffic. Fifth has a number of retail businesses in that area, and I believe there might be an office building or two within a couple of blocks of Ray's. The diagram (Exhibit 1) that you showed me looks to be accurate.

I often ate at Ray's Steakhouse—about three times a week. It was a good place to take customers because it was centrally located and, despite its name, had a varied and good menu. Ray's had valet parking—you just pulled into the driveway next to the restaurant, and one of the carhops took your car back to parking. The valet who usually took my car is Alex. I don't know Alex's last name. Because I was a regular, it wasn't unusual for Alex to have my car waiting for me in one of the street spaces right in front of Ray's. I don't know if Alex did this for other regulars, but they did it for me. I guess I'm a decent tipper. I always gave Alex five bucks when I left off the car and another five bucks when I picked it up. If I gave Alex a ten that day, it was a mistake.

As I said, I met Jordan Anderson at the restaurant. I had offered to drive them there, but Jordan said that they had some errands to do in that part of town, so they wanted to drive their own car. We had a pleasant lunch. I don't remember what they ate, but I had my usual—a chicken Caesar salad and coffee. I also had a glass of chardonnay with my salad. That, too, is my usual lunch beverage. I do not consider myself a heavy drinker, but I do enjoy a martini before dinner each evening. Yes, I sometimes also have wine with dinner. No, I never have a martini at lunch. I don't believe in drinking hard liquor when I'm working. The wine at lunch that day certainly had no effect on me. I was perfectly sober. I don't remember if Jordan had any alcohol at lunch.

The lunch lasted until about 2:00 p.m. I paid the check and thanked Jordan for taking the time to eat with me and for their assistance with my sales efforts with Abbott, and we said our goodbyes at the restaurant door. I offered Jordan a ride back to Abbott's, but Jordan reminded me that they had their car and that it was parked on Fifth Street, a short distance east of the restaurant. As usual, my car was parked outside the restaurant. There was a car parked both in front and behind my car. I got the keys from Alex, tipped them, and got into my car.

I got into my car, a YR-3 Cadillac four-door sedan, and started the engine. Because it was a warm day, the air conditioning came on automatically. My phone connected to my car speakers via Bluetooth and that was playing, also. No, it wasn't loud music. It was a podcast.

Q: Tell me everything you did after you started your car.

A: What I would usually do. I put my seatbelt on, backed up enough so that I could pull into the middle lane, checked my mirrors, and then pulled out. Just as I eased into the center lane, I caught a flash out of the corner of my eye of something very fast, and then, boom, it rammed into the front left side of my car.

Q: That was Jackie Fulbright on his motorcycle?

A: Yes. He went flying off the cycle and landed about twenty feet down the street. I immediately stopped my car and ran up to him where he was lying on the pavement. He was unconscious on the pavement. He did not have his helmet on, and I don't think he had it on when he hit my car. It all happened so fast, I can't be sure, but I don't think he had it on.

Q: Did you actually see the cycle before impact?

A: Only like a whoosh out of the corner of my eye. But from how fast everything happened, he must have been going very fast.

Q: But you couldn't estimate the precise speed?

A: I saw a blur, like I said—a whoosh. My best guess is that he was going at least fifty.

Q: But that's just a guess?

A: I didn't have a radar gun with me, if that's what you're asking.

Q: So you don't know his speed for certain?

A: For absolute certain, no. No, I didn't hear him approach me, either, I guess, because I had on the air conditioner on high-speed fan and the podcast was on. He just came out of nowhere.

By the time I got to him—I know now he was John Fulbright, the plaintiff—Jordan was already there. I asked Jordan something like, where did he come from, but Jordan didn't answer. I really did not see the motorcycle until right as it ran into my car. I immediately called 911 on my cell phone. I also called the office to tell them what happened.

The police officer and ambulance arrived almost immediately. After the officer helped to get Fulbright into the ambulance, the officer talked to Jordan, Alex, and myself, and maybe some other people who saw the accident. I told the officer what happened, as did Jordan and Alex. I think we all estimated that Fulbright was traveling about fifty miles an hour. I believe the speed limit on Fifth Street is twenty-five miles an hour, although I'll have to admit that usually the traffic along there travels at closer to thirty or thirty-five. No matter, he was certainly going faster than that.

After we talked to the officer, he asked if we could give him signed statements. I told him that I had a 2:30 appointment I was already late for. It was about thirty minutes away, so, yes, by the time the accident happened, I was running a few minutes late. The officer let me go, and I promised to go into the police department the next day to give a statement. By the time I got to my client's office, he was in his next appointment, so I didn't get to see him. Because I was so shaken up by this accident, I just went home instead of going back to Americraft.

When I got home, I emailed Aaron Morrow, Americraft's assistant sales manager. Yes, Exhibit 25 is my email and his response and my reply. No, of course I didn't think I had PTSD. It was just a bad joke. In fact, my spouse and I went out to dinner that night. We went to Ruth's Chris. Yes, I probably did have a martini.

Yes, I called Americraft's lawyer after the accident, and he told me that because people were so lawsuit crazy, I was not to talk to anyone about the accident and not to sign anything, so I did go to the police station the next day, but I told them that I couldn't give them a statement. Not that it makes any difference. I had already told the officer exactly what I told you today about how the accident happened.

I was definitely on a business lunch with Jordan on July 20, YR-2. I'm sure I put in for the lunch on my expense account. The document you showed me (Exhibit 6) is a portion of my expense account report for the month of July YR-2, and yes, it shows that I put in for and was paid for that lunch. I have to put in these reports every week, and then I am reimbursed for my expenses. They are sent back to me, and I keep them in my files. That's company policy.

I just give my administrative assistant my credit card receipts, and she fills out the report and submits it with the receipts. Then, about a week later, I get a copy with the approvals for the expenses along with a reimbursement check. If our accounting department doesn't approve an expense, then I don't get reimbursed. Yes, the escort service expense was denied. No, it wasn't a typical expense, just something that particular client asked for.

I am very sorry that this young man was injured, but it was not my fault. I'm a very careful driver. And anyway, he came out of nowhere and was going so fast when he hit me, there was nothing I could to do to avoid the accident.

I have given full and complete answers to all of your questions. If I remember anything further about what you've asked, I'll tell my lawyer so that she can tell you.

I have read the foregoing, and it is a true and accurate transcription of my deposition given on January 13, YR-0, in my office at Americraft Industries in Nita City.

Jamie Parker

Jamie Parker

Subscribed and sworn before me the 13th day of January, YR-0.

Harry Gibbons

Harry Gibbons

Notary

Deposition of Jordan Anderson

My name is Jordan Anderson. I live at 12 Coventry Court in Nita City. I am twenty-eight years old and work as purchasing assistant to the president of Abbott Aluminum Company, David Slater. I am a YR-6 graduate of the University of Nita, where I received a bachelor's degree in business administration. I have worked in my current position since graduation.

My job at Abbott Aluminum is to advise Mr. Slater on the full range of business decisions he has to make, and in particular with respect to the purchasing of materials we need in our manufacturing operations. I am also involved in the decisions made concerning our entry into new markets. For example, I was instrumental in our YR-4 decision to manufacture and market aluminum parts to the automobile industry. That market now represents 20 percent of our business. Other than Mr. Slater, there are only two other managers, one for operations and one for marketing.

Yes, I know Jamie Parker. Parker is the sales representative for Americraft Industries. Americraft is a Nita City company that manufactures a full range of industrial machinery. We have done business with Americraft and Parker on numerous occasions. Americraft has assisted us in designing the machinery we've needed in various expansion projects over the years. We have been very satisfied with their products and have received excellent service from them during my time with Abbott.

Although Jamie is a perfectly good sales representative, Jamie can be a bit pushy at times—you know, typical salesperson. Jamie frequently asked me out to lunch and dinner, even though I don't need to be entertained to consider purchasing products and services from Americraft. I generally decline Jamie's invitations because I have a busy work schedule and don't generally have the time for a long, social lunch, and would frankly prefer to dine with my family and friends than with a business associate. I always put Jamie off in a nice way, but I was always very clear. Jamie didn't seem to get the point, so in July of YR-2—I believe it was the twentieth—I agreed to go to lunch with Jamie. I drove my own car rather than accepting Jamie's offer to drive.

We met for lunch at Ray's Steakhouse, which was located on Fifth Street between Clay and Forest streets in Nita City. Fifth Street in that part of town is a retail store center, although there might be an office building near there. I say that only because there are also a lot of restaurants in the area, and restaurants in downtown areas are usually built close to office buildings so they can cash in on the lunch business. The diagram (Exhibit 1) you've showed me looks to be accurate to that area.

I parked my car on Fifth Street just before Clay, about half a block east of Ray's Steakhouse. I had never been there before that day, so I did not realize that they had valet parking. Fifth is a three-lane, one-way road going east. The southernmost lane is used for parking, although I know that I've driven along there when all three lanes were available for traffic. I believe that the speed limit there is the same as every other street in the downtown area—twenty-five miles per hour.

I met Jamie at the restaurant at approximately 12:30 p.m. Lunch was pleasant. I don't recall what I ate, but I do remember that the food was good. I had an iced tea to drink. I know that only because that's all I ever drink at lunch.

Q: Do you remember what Parker had to drink at lunch?

A: Yes, Jamie had two martinis.

Q: Are you sure of that?

A: Yes, I remember because I thought that was a lot to drink in the middle of the day.

Q: Gin or vodka?

A: I don't recall.

Q: Olive or twist?

A: I don't recall that either.

Q: Up or on the rocks?

A: Up. I remember they came in a traditional martini glass.

Q: Like the glass shown in Exhibit 22?

A: Yes.

Q: Did the two martinis appear to affect Parker?

A: Not really. Jamie was a little loose-tongued, but that was usually their style.

Q: In all the times you'd seen Jamie Parker at Abbott, had you ever suspected that they'd been drinking?

A: Never.

Lunch lasted until a little after 2:00 p.m. I remember that Jamie told me they'd have to go because they were running a little late for their next appointment. We left the restaurant, and Parker pointed to their car that was parked in front of the restaurant and offered me a ride back to the office because it was on their way. I reminded Jamie that I had driven myself and pointed down the street to where my car was parked. We said our goodbyes, and I walked toward my car. Just as I reached my car and was putting my key in the door on the driver's side, I heard the roar of a motorcycle coming from back down Fifth. I looked up to hear a crash and saw the rider of the bike flying through the air in my direction. I did not see the bike before impact, but it obviously had run into the front left side of Jamie's Cadillac.

I can't say whether the rider had on a helmet as he was flying through the air because it all happened so fast, but he certainly didn't have one on when I ran over to where he landed in the street. He landed about twenty feet down Fifth Street from where he hit Parker's car. I got there first, and Parker got there within a few seconds. The motorcycle rider, who looked to be a teenager, was unconscious. As Parker got there, they looked at me and said, "Where the hell did he come from?" Then Jamie immediately called 911 on their cell phone.

A police officer and ambulance arrived within a few minutes. The teenager was taken away. The cop asked if I would give a statement. Even though I was in a hurry, I waited to talk to him. He also talked with the valet from Ray's Steakhouse and Parker at the same time. A person also approached him and gave him a motorcycle helmet they said belonged to "Jackie." The officer talked with that person as well. I told the officer just what I've told you today. He asked how fast we thought the bike was going before the accident. I don't know who said what first, but the three of us agreed that it must have been about fifty miles per hour. I told the officer that I had a lot of experience with motorcycles, given that both my brother and I raced them when we were in our late teens. Even though I didn't see the bike before impact, based on the sound, I told him that I figured that the bike must have been going fifty miles per hour. I have no reason to change that estimate today.

I now know that the teenager who was hurt was John Fulbright. I'm a pretty avid sports fan and recognize his name as the star quarterback of one of the Nita City high schools. I've heard that because of this accident, he's never been able to play again. That's too bad, because from what I've heard and read, he was a special football player with a bright future.

Jamie Parker is still the Americraft representative who handles our account at Abbott. We continue to deal with Jamie because Americraft has a good product line and gives us good prices. Jamie also pays attention to our account and has done a good job in fulfilling some special requirements in terms of speed of delivery. Of course I've seen Jamie since the accident, but I can't say that we've ever really discussed the accident. We might have, but I just don't remember.

I have given full and complete answers to your questions. If I think of anything further I'll contact you, but I think that's unlikely.

I have read the foregoing, and it is a true and accurate transcript of my deposition given on January 17, YR-0, in the office of plaintiff's counsel.

Jordan Anderson

Jordan Anderson

Subscribed and sworn before me this 17th day of January, YR-0.

Harry Gibbons

Harry Gibbons

Notary

Deposition of Alex Markham

My name is Alex Markham. I am twenty-six years old. I live at 1300 Forest, Apartment 17, Nita City. I am a night-school student at Nita Technical College, where I am majoring in computer science. I hope to get my BS degree in a couple of years, if things go along like they have been. I also work as a valet at Ray's Steakhouse, which is now located on Adams Street in Nita City. Ray's used to be on Fifth Street by Forest, but that's now some Asian fusion restaurant. I work the lunch shift from 11:30 a.m. to 2:30 p.m. every day except Sunday, and the dinner shift on Fridays and Saturdays when I don't have any classes. This leaves me plenty of time to study. I've been working there for about four years, since I got out of the Army in YR-4, and I've always worked the same shifts. The hourly pay is just a little better than minimum wage, but the tips are pretty good, especially on Friday and Saturday nights when the patrons get a little liquor in them. Yes, Jamie Parker is still a good customer.

I graduated from high school in YR-8 and immediately enlisted in the Army. I didn't know what I wanted to do with my life. I thought the service was a good idea. The Army was okay, but I didn't want to make it my career, so I took my honorable discharge in YR-4. Yes, I was deployed overseas. Despite all their promises, I never got the kind of high-tech training you hear them talk about on television, so I enrolled in Nita Tech when I got out. I started to work at Ray's to cover my expenses that were more than the amount that was covered by my G.I. Bill.

Jamie Parker has been one of my regulars at Ray's ever since I started working there. Parker has lunch there a couple times a week and sometimes comes in with their spouse for dinner on the weekends. Most times Parker has a guest when they come in for lunch. Parker usually shows up around 12:30 and has a long lunch until about 2:00 or 2:30. Parker seems to be a nice person, always making jokes, and Parker's a good tipper. Parker gives me five dollars when I park their car and five dollars again when they pick it up. After I got to know Parker's usual schedule, I started to bring their car around and park it right in front when it was about the time for them to come out of the restaurant. Parker seemed to like that, so that's what I always do.

I was working on July 20 of YR-2 when that kid ran into the side of Parker's car and nearly killed himself. There was nothing that Parker could do. The kid came speeding around that truck and just slammed into Parker's car.

At the time of the accident, I was standing right in front of Ray's, so I got a good view of everything that happened. Ray's was located on the south side of Fifth Street. Fifth is a three-lane road that goes one way, eastbound. The lane in front of Ray's was used for parking, except during rush hour. Ray's had a driveway off of Fifth that leads up to the entrance to the restaurant. That's also where the valets took the cars from the patrons to park in the lot behind the restaurant. When the accident happened, I had just given Parker the car keys and was watching Parker and Parker's lunch companion walk to their to their cars.

When Parker came out of the restaurant, Parker saw their Cadillac parked out in front and gave me a big smile. Parker seemed a little more animated than usual. No, Parker didn't appear drunk or anything like that. Also, when Parker tipped me when they were leaving, they gave me a ten-dollar bill instead of the usual five, so Parker must have been in a good mood. Exhibit 10 shows the entrance to what was then Ray's Steakhouse. The awning is the same except that it now says Yank Sing. Parker's car was parked directly in front of the awning that extends towards Fifth Street. Exhibits 11 and 12 also show where Ray's used to be. Anyhow, I watched Parker wave goodbye to their friend and get into their Cadillac. Parker's friend walked down the street, cutting between two cars to get to the driver's side of a car parked about half of a block down Fifth Street.

Parker got into the car, started it, and began to pull out. It was then that the motorcycle came around a truck that was in the far north lane and into the center lane. I don't know whether I first heard the roar of the bike or saw it, it all happened so fast. Neither the kid nor Parker had a chance. The kid was going so fast that he couldn't swerve, and I doubt that Parker ever saw him, so Parker couldn't have gotten out of the way. The kid hit the front left side of Parker's Cadillac and went flying through the air.

Based on what I saw, I'd have to say that the kid was going about fifty miles an hour. The speed limit on Fifth is twenty-five miles an hour. I can't be absolutely certain, but I don't think the kid was even wearing a helmet. I don't remember seeing one on his head, and he certainly didn't have one on when he landed up the street.

Both Parker and Parker's friend ran to try to help the kid. Parker called 911 right away. The kid was knocked out. To be honest, it's a miracle he didn't kill himself, considering how fast he was going.

Within a couple of minutes, a cop and an ambulance showed up. They loaded the kid into the ambulance, and it took off. The cop stayed behind and took statements from me, Parker, Parker's friend, and a person who came up and told the cop that they'd seen the accident and handed the cop a motorcycle helmet. I told the cop just what I told you today. There wasn't much question about what happened. As we talked to the cop, it was pretty clear that Parker, Parker's friend, and I saw it about the same way. The cop asked me if I'd mind signing a statement about what I saw, and I agreed to come into the police station the next morning to sign a statement, which I did. The piece of paper you just showed me (Exhibit 4) is the statement I signed.

I didn't see Parker for a month or so, and the next time I saw Parker they were driving a new Cadillac. Parker made some kind of joke about it being a hard way to get a new car or something like that. I asked Parker if they were all right, and they said they were. That's the last time I had any conversation with anyone about it until about six months after the accident, when some guy from Parker's insurance company came out to talk to me about what happened. He wanted to know all about the accident, but seemed especially concerned about whether the kid had on his helmet. He said the kid hurt his head and was claiming that it had caused him to have a serious medical problem. I told him what I told you. I can't be sure whether he had the helmet on or not, but I don't remember seeing the helmet on his head. That's the last time I had any conversation with anyone about this accident before today.

I have given full and complete answers to all of your questions. If I remember anything more, I'll make changes on the transcript of this deposition when I get to read it.

I have read the foregoing, and it is a true and accurate transcription of my deposition given on February 17, YR-0, in the offices of defendant's counsel.

Alex Markham
Alex Markham

Subscribed and sworn before me the 17th day of February, YR-0.

Harry Gibbons
Harry Gibbons

Notary

DEPOSITION OF TATUM HARRIS

My name is Tatum Harris. I am an assistant football coach at Nita State University. I am in charge of offense, particularly the quarterbacks and wide receivers. I started at Nita State this year. Before that, I was head football coach at Nita City Central High School for five years. Before that, I was a graduate assistant in the football program at the University of Texas. Before that, I was an undergraduate at Texas. I was a tight end on the UT football team for three years. My freshman year I was red-shirted, but I played the next three years. The last two years I played I was a starter, at least until I blew my knee out in the A&M game. I had surgery and went through rehab, but I was never able to play after the injury. I obtained my bachelor's degree at the University of Texas and also obtained a master's degree in secondary education while I worked as a graduate assistant in the football program.

I coached Jackie Fulbright when he played for Nita City Central. I have never seen a better high school quarterback anywhere. Jackie had a great arm, a cool head, and could run a 4.7 forty. He could throw a football sixty yards with accuracy. He is extremely intelligent and a hard worker.

Yes, I remember Jackie's last practice at Central. I made it full contact, including the quarterbacks, because the kids needed some game-feel before the season started. One of our defensive ends eluded his block and hit Jackie from his blind side. Jackie stayed on the ground without moving for a couple of seconds, and I rushed onto the field to see how he was. By the time I got to him, he was moving his head and asking what happened. He was able to get up with some help, and he made it off the field slowly, but under his own power.

I kept Jackie out of the rest of the practice, and I told him he'd have to see the school nurse the next morning to be checked for a concussion. Jackie seemed to understand, but he wanted to get back on to the field. His speech seemed a little slow, but by the time we finished practice, he was back to his old self. I really don't know whether he was momentarily unconscious before I got to him on the field.

Yes, I agree that Jackie got his bell rung that day. Yes, I understand that getting one's bell rung may constitute a concussion. No, I've never seen a player get his bell rung and then have problems with remembering things or not being able to make decisions and read the defense appropriately, just because he got hit.

Exhibit 7 is Nita State's quarterback evaluation memo for the recruiting year that would have been Jackie's senior year. This is a confidential record similar to the record that every major college football program keeps for every position. I have obtained permission to make it public because so much time has gone by that it can't matter any longer to Nita State's recruiting competition. Besides, Nita State hired a new head coach the year following what would have been Jackie's senior year in high school. Nita State finished 3-8 during that year, and they fired their coach and his whole staff right after the season was over. They hired Coach Bryant about a month later, and he hired me about two months after that. We were 8-3 this past year.

I have given full and complete answers to all of your questions. I will read my deposition for accuracy when it is transcribed.

I have read the foregoing, and it is a true and accurate transcription of my deposition given on February 2, YR-0, in the offices of the plaintiff's attorney.

Tatum Harris
Tatum Harris

Subscribed and sworn before me this 2nd day of February, YR-0.

Harry Gibbons
Harry Gibbons

Notary

Deposition of Reagan Flanagan

My name is Reagan Flanagan. I am thirty-eight years old. I am the chief financial officer of Mangez-A-Trois, Inc. We operate twenty-two restaurants in this region of the country. We have a variety of restaurant types, but most are moderately upscale. Ray's Steakhouse in Nita City is one of our properties. Ray's was located on Fifth Street until the end of YR-1. We then moved it about a mile away. We moved because we wanted a bigger place with an open kitchen and better parking.

In YR-2, all our restaurants used the E-Serve software system for tracking orders. Each server would enter the relevant information for each table on a touchscreen monitor. That included the table number, the number of guests at the table, and what was ordered. The system would send the information to the bar or the kitchen where the drinks or food would be prepared. When an order was ready, the bartender or chef would signal the server on a vibrating pager, and the server would pick up the order and deliver it to the table.

The system also printed the check for each table and added the sales tax, which in Nita is 6 percent. The system stored all its information on our servers. We used that information to determine which items were selling and which ones were not. No, we didn't include the tip because many customers tip with cash and because, for tax purposes, most servers prefer to estimate what their tips are.

In YR-1, we changed software to a new product that allows us to obtain chain-wide information. E-Serve was a good system, but we could only access information property by property. Yes, we found it pretty reliable. It crashed occasionally like any software, but we were generally happy with it.

I was able to query the E-Serve data that is still on our servers for July 20, YR-2. In response to your subpoena, one of our techies asked to see the records for the lunch hour (for Ray's, 11:30–3:00) for all tables of two persons where a chicken caesar salad or a martini was ordered. Exhibit 23 is the report that E-Serve created.

That's correct, there was no two-person table where we sold a chicken caesar salad and two martinis. The closest is table number two, where we sold a salad, a well martini, and a well Manhattan. "Well" means that the customer did not specify the brand of liquor, so we use a nonpremium label. Where the customer specifies a brand, that is listed as a premium drink.

There were two tables where we sold a chicken caesar salad and some chardonnay. One table ordered two glasses of Kendall Jackson chardonnay, and the other ordered one glass of house chardonnay and a Bass Ale.

Yes, I understand that someone has claimed that one of our customers had two martinis and a chicken caesar salad at lunch on July 20, YR-2. If that is what happened, it should have shown up on the E-Serve report. Yes, I suppose that the report could be mistaken if the server punched in a Manhattan instead of a martini and the bartender made a change without entering it on the computer. In other words, if the server went to pick up the drink and saw it was a Manhattan, not a martini, the server would ask the bartender to make the change, and the bartender might well have poured the Manhattan out and made a new martini without entering it on the computer. That would have been quicker and, because the charge for the two drinks is the same, would not have affected any internal accounting. No, I have never worked as a bartender, but I spend a lot of time in our restaurants, and I know that during busy times the bartenders like to do what is quickest.

I checked with our current wait staff, but nobody has any recollection of having served Parker and Parker's guest that particular day.

I have read the foregoing, and it is a true and accurate transcription of my deposition given on March 9, YR-0, in the office of plaintiff's counsel.

Reagan Flanagan
Reagan Flanagan

Subscribed and sworn before me this 9th day of March, YR-0.

Harry Gibbons
Harry Gibbons

Notary

Jury Instructions

The law you are to apply to this case is contained in these instructions, and it is your duty to follow them. You must consider them as a whole, and not pick out one or some instructions and disregard others.

Sympathy or prejudice must not influence your decision.

I have not meant to indicate any opinion about the facts by my rulings, conduct, or remarks during the trial. But if you think I have, you should disregard it because you are the sole judges of the facts.

You shall consider all of the evidence bearing on any fact without regard to which party produced the evidence.

A fact may be proven directly by a witness or indirectly by other facts or circumstances from which it reasonably follows according to common experience. This indirect evidence is called circumstantial evidence, and it should be considered by you in the same manner as direct evidence.

In determining which witnesses you will believe and what weight you will give to their testimony, you may take into account each witness's ability and opportunity to observe; the witness's memory; manner while testifying; and any interest, bias, or prejudice they may have.

I shall now give you the definitions of some important legal terms, which I shall use later.

1) When I use the term "negligence" with respect to the defendant's conduct, I mean the failure to do something that a reasonably careful person would do or the doing of something that a reasonably careful person would not do under the circumstances that you find existed in this case.

2) When I use the words "ordinary care," I mean the care a reasonably careful person would use under the circumstances that you find existed in this case.

3) It was the duty of the plaintiff, in connection with the accident that is the subject of this case, to use ordinary care for his own safety.

4) It was the duty of the defendant in connection with the accident that is the subject of this case, to use ordinary care for the safety of the plaintiff.

5) When I use the terms "negligence" or "contributory negligence" with respect to the plaintiff's conduct, I mean the plaintiff's failure to use ordinary care for his own safety, which proximately contributed to his injury.

6) When I use the words "proximate cause," I mean, first, that there must have been a connection between the conduct of the defendant that plaintiff claims was negligent and the injury of which the plaintiff complains, and second, that the occurrence that is claimed to have produced that injury was a natural or foreseeable result of such conduct of the defendant.

7) When I use the words "proximately contributed," I mean, first, that there must have been a connection between that conduct of the plaintiff that defendant claims was negligent and the injury of which plaintiff complains, and second, that the occurrence that is claimed to have produced that injury was a natural or foreseeable result of such conduct of the plaintiff.

8) There may be more than one proximate cause. To be a proximate cause, the claimed negligence of the defendant need not be the only cause nor the last cause. A cause may be proximate although it and another cause act at the same time or in combination to produce the occurrence.

9) I shall now explain to you the burden of proof that the law places on the parties to establish their respective claims. When I say that a party has the burden of proof or use the expression "if you find" or "if you decide," I mean that the evidence must satisfy you that the proposition on which that party has the burden of proof has been established by evidence that outweighs the evidence against it. You must consider all the evidence, regardless of which party produced it.

10) The plaintiff has the burden of proof on each of the following propositions:

a) that the plaintiff suffered an injury;
b) that the defendant was negligent in one or more of the ways claimed by the plaintiff; and
c) that the negligence of the defendant was a proximate cause of the plaintiff 's injury.

11) The defendant has the burden of proof on the defendant's claim that the plaintiff was negligent in one or more of the ways claimed by the defendant and that such negligence was a proximate contributing cause of plaintiff's injury.

12) The verdict will be for the plaintiff if he was injured and if the defendant was negligent and the defendant's negligence was a proximate cause of plaintiff's injury.

13) The verdict will be for the defendant if plaintiff was not injured or if the defendant was not negligent, or if defendant was negligent, defendant's negligence was not a proximate cause of plaintiff's injury.

14) If you find that each party was negligent and that the negligence of each party was a proximate cause of the plaintiff's injury, then you must determine what degree of such negligence, expressed as a percentage, can be attributed to the plaintiff. Negligence on the part of the plaintiff does not bar recovery by the plaintiff, but the percentage of negligence attributable to the plaintiff will be used by the court to reduce the amount of damages the plaintiff is entitled to recover.

The court will furnish a special verdict form to assist you in your duties. Your answers to the questions in the special verdict form will provide the basis on which this case will be resolved.

IN THE SUPERIOR COURT OF NITA COUNTY
STATE OF NITA

JOHN FULBRIGHT, Plaintiff v. AMERICRAFT INDUSTRIES and JAMIE PARKER, Defendants.	)))))))))	 Civil Action No. 23-1234

VERDICT FORM

We, the jury, make the following answers to the questions submitted by the court:

QUESTION NO. 1: Was the defendant negligent?

ANSWER: ________ (Yes or No)

If your answer is "no," do not answer any further questions.

QUESTION NO. 2: Was the defendant's negligence a proximate cause of injury or damage to the plaintiff?

ANSWER: ________ (Yes or No)

QUESTION NO. 3: Was the plaintiff negligent?

ANSWER: ________ (Yes or No)

If your answer is "no," do not answer any further questions.

QUESTION NO. 4: Was the plaintiff's negligence a proximate cause of injury or damage to the plaintiff?

ANSWER: ________ (Yes or No)

If your answer is "no," do not answer any further questions.

QUESTION NO. 5: Using 100 percent as the total combined negligence that proximately caused the injury or damage to the plaintiff, what percentage of such negligence is attributable to the plaintiff?

ANSWER: ________ percent

Signed,

____

Foreperson

EXHIBITS

Exhibit 1

Diagram of Accident Scene

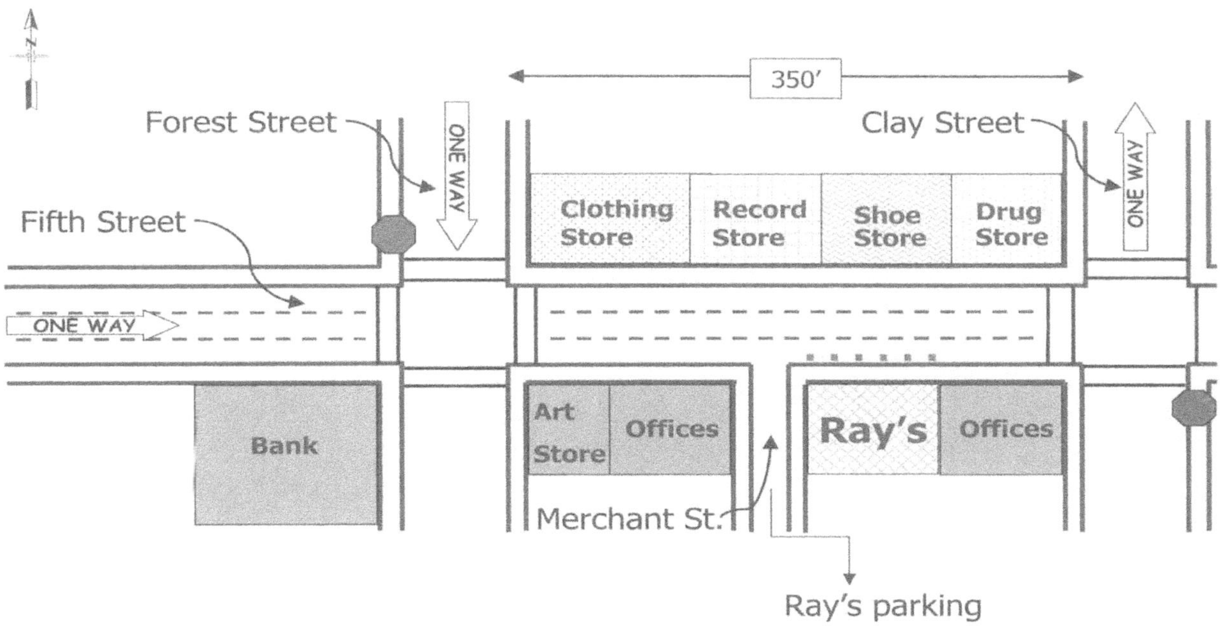

▪ ▪ ▪ ▪ ▪ ▪ No parking

Exhibit 2

OFFICIAL TRAFFIC ACCIDENT REPORT

DEPARTMENT NAME: Nita City P.D.

ACCIDENT LOCATION

COUNTY: Nita | CITY: Nita | ACCIDENT DATE: 7/20/YR-2 | TIME: 2:20 p.m.

STREET NAME: Fifth Street | FT N S E W | INTERSECTION: Between Clay and Forest

ACCIDENT CONDITIONS

WEATHER: (1) CLEAR/CLOUDY 3 RAIN 2 FOG 4 SNOW | LIGHT: (1) DAY 3 ST LTS 2 DAWN/DUSK 4 DARK | ROAD SURFACE: (1) DRY 3 SNOW OR ICE 2 WET 4 OTHER | TOTAL LANES 3 | 1.DIVIDED 2 LIMITED ACCESS 3 OTHER | Y N CONSTRUCTION ZONE | (Y) N INVESTIGATED AT SCENE

VEHICLE DRIVER NO 1

STATE: Nita | DRIVER'S LICENSE: F1350492721808 | DOB: 2/2/YR-17 | HAZARDOUS ACTION/CITATION (Y) N: Speed too fast/No helmet | HELMET Y (N)

DRIVER'S NAME First: John | MI: C | Last: Fulbright | ADDRESS: 2942 Rivington | City: Nita City | State: Nita | AGE: 17 | SEX: M | INJ.: A

YEAR: YR-4 | MAKE: Honda | MODEL: Aero | TRAILER: N | REGISTRATION: BFP092 | YR/STATE: YR-0 NT | VIN: | REMOVED TO/BY: Hal's Towing

Y N HAZ. CITATION / Y N OTHER CITATION | Y N DRIVER RE-EXAM / Y (N) VISION OBSCTRUCT. | Y (N) VEHICLE DEFECT / Y N VEHICLE DRIVEABLE | Y N FUEL LEAKAGE / Y N VEHICLE FIRE | IMPACT SEVERITY: 2

RESTRAINTS BY OCCUPANT'S POS.	NAME	ADDRESS	POS	AGE	SEX	INJ	HELMET Y N
1 2 3							Y N
4 5 6							Y N

TOTAL OCCUPANTS: 1 | LOCAL OWNER/USER PHONE | INSURANCE CO | AGENCY PHONE | INJURED TAKEN TO/BY: General Hospital

VEHICLE DRIVER NO 2

STATE: Nita | DRIVER'S LICENSE: P480927460011 | DOB: 8/28/YR-41 | HAZARDOUS ACTION/CITATION (Y) N: Improper Lane Change | HELMET Y N

DRIVER'S NAME First: Jamie | MI: M. | Last: Parker | ADDRESS: 4211 | City: Granger | State: Nita City | AGE: 40 | SEX: M | INJ.: –

YEAR: YR-3 | MAKE: Cadillac | MODEL: | TRAILER: | REGISTRATION: CBA711 | YR/STATE: YR-1 NT | VIN: | REMOVED TO/BY: Driver

Y N HAZ. CITATION / Y N OTHER CITATION | Y N DRIVER RE-EXAM / Y N VISION OBSCTRUCT. | Y N VEHICLE DEFECT / Y N VEHICLE DRIVEABLE | Y N FUEL LEAKAGE / Y N VEHICLE FIRE | IMPACT SEVERITY

RESTRAINTS BY OCCUPANT'S POS.	NAME	ADDRESS	POS	AGE	INJ	HELMET Y N
	Alex Markham		W	24	–	Y N
1 2 3	Jordan Anderson		W	26	–	Y N
4 5 6	Blake Brown		W	38	–	Y N

TOTAL OCCUPANTS | LOCAL OWNER/USER PHONE: Americraft Industries Inc | INSURANCE CO | AGENCY PHONE | INJURED TAKEN TO/BY

ACCIDENT DESCRIPTION AND REMARKS (EXPLAIN)

#1 (cycle) came around truck at high rate of speed as #2 was pulling into middle lane

See witness statements attached

No skid marks. Driver #1 thrown approximately 20 feet

REPORTED: DATE: 7/20/YR-2 | TIME: 20:22 | INVESTIGATORS: T. O'Brien | CASE NUMBER: BB2201

DAMAGE TO PROPERTY OTHER THAN VEHICLES: None

Exhibit 3

Supplemental Police Report

Interview with Jordan Anderson

Jordan Anderson is twenty-six years old and is employed as a purchasing assistant to the president of Abbott Aluminum Company in Nita City. Anderson had eaten lunch at Ray's Steakhouse with Jamie Parker, who is a business associate, and was about to enter their car parked on Fifth Street when they heard a motorcycle rev its engine and crash into left front quarter panel of Parker's Cadillac. Motorcyclist flies through the air and lands on pavement. Estimates speed of motorcycle at 50 mph. Uncertain as to whether motorcyclist was wearing a helmet when impact occurred. Motorcyclist did not have helmet on when he came to rest on Fifth Street.

Witness reports that Parker had two martinis to drink during lunch, but that Parker did not appear to be impaired in any way. Requested that Anderson sign a statement, but witness declined due to busy schedule.

Interview with Blake Brown

Witness is thirty-eight years old. Witness approached officer while he was interviewing other witnesses. Handed helmet to officer and asked that it be returned to motorcyclist, who witness referred to as "Jackie." Helmet has been made to resemble football helmet. Has number 8 on the front. Witness states witness found helmet on north side of Fifth between point of impact and where motorcyclist came to rest.

Witness saw motorcyclist traveling in northern lane of Fifth Street wave at witness and then change lanes from behind a truck into center lane of Fifth, whereupon Cadillac pulled away from curb quickly and into path of motorcycle. Witness unable to estimate speed in mph, but states that motorcycle was not going very fast. Witness is certain that motorcyclist was wearing helmet.

Witness identifies motorcyclist as Jackie Fulbright, who, according to witness, is a star high school football player.

Interview with Jamie Parker

Witness was pulling away from parking place in front of Ray's Steakhouse when motorcycle ran into the front left quarter panel of witness's YR-3 Cadillac. Witness had just eased into center lane of Fifth Street when Cadillac was struck by motorcyclist who was traveling at a high rate of speed. Estimates speed of motorcycle at 50 mph. States that they do not believe that motorcyclist was wearing a helmet.

Witness states that they had lunch at Ray's Steakhouse. Admits to having one drink during lunch. Does not appear intoxicated in any way. Witness states they have an important appointment and asks to leave before any more in-depth interview. Agrees to come into station next day to give a formal statement. Appears at station on 7/21 but declines to give written statement on advice of counsel. Witness is otherwise cooperative.

Interview with Alex Markham

Interviewed witness at scene. Witness has given signed statement (attached).

Interview with John Fulbright

Interviewed witness at General Hospital. Witness has given signed statement (attached).

Exhibit 4

Alex Markham Witness Statement

I, Alex Markham, am twenty-four years old and live at 1300 Forest, Apartment 17, in Nita City, Nita. I am a part-time student at Nita Technical College, and I also work as a carhop at Ray's Steakhouse on Fifth Street in Nita City.

I was working on July 20, YR-2, at approximately 2:00 p.m. I witnessed an accident where a motorcycle collided with the front left of a Cadillac. I do not know the motorcyclist. The Cadillac was driven by one of our regular customers, Jamie Parker.

Parker had lunch at Ray's on July 20, arriving at approximately 12:15 p.m. and leaving at approximately 2:00 p.m. Parker came alone to the restaurant and I parked the car. I later moved the car to a parking space in front of the restaurant so that Parker could leave as soon as they finished lunch.

Parker got into the car, started it, and pulled out onto Fifth Street. At that time, I heard the roar of a motorcycle and looked up to see a motorcycle going fast. It changed lanes around a truck in the far north lane of Fifth, went into Parker's lane, and crashed into the front left corner panel. The motorcyclist went flying. I don't think the motorcyclist was wearing a helmet because he didn't have it on when I saw him lying on the pavement, but it could have flown off when he hit. I just don't know. It happened so fast.

I don't think there was anything that Parker could have done to avoid the motorcycle. Given the speed and the fact that he came around the truck, I'm not sure there's anything the motorcyclist could have done either.

I have read the above five paragraphs. They are an accurate transcription of the statement I have given to Officer O'Brien of the Nita City Police Department. The statement is, to the best of my knowledge, true and accurate.

Alex Markham

Alex Markham
July 21, 2022

Tracy O'Brien

Witness:
Tracy O'Brien
NCPD

John Fulbright Witness Statement

I, John Fulbright, am seventeen years old and live with my parents at 2492 Rivington Road in Nita City. I am about to enter into my senior year at Nita Central High School. I am currently employed as a playground director for the summer.

On July 20, YR-2, at approximately 2:00 p.m., I was involved in an accident on Fifth Street between Forest and Clay in Nita City. At that time, my motorcycle collided with the front left quarter panel of a Cadillac that was pulling into the center lane of Fifth Street. I was traveling at about 30 or 35 mph on Fifth Street, a 25-mph road, when the accident happened. The Cadillac pulled away from a parking space on the south side of Fifth Street when I ran into it. I could not avoid the collision.

After we hit, I went flying through the air. The next thing I can remember, I woke up in General Hospital. I am told that I didn't have my helmet on when I struck the pavement. I can't remember, but I don't believe that because I always wear a helmet when I ride my motorcycle.

I have read the above three paragraphs. It is an accurate transcription of the statement I said to Officer O'Brien. To the best of my knowledge, the statement is true and accurate.

John Fulbright

John Fulbright
July 21, 2022

Tracy O'Brien

Witness:
Tracy O'Brien
NCPD

Exhibit 6

Americraft Industries
Expense Report

J. Parker—Week of July 19–23, YR-2

YR-2	CLIENT	LOCATION	AMOUNT	APPROVAL
19-Jul	BMI	Ray's	$38.50	pmn
	P McCune			
19-Jul	Staff Dinner	Chop House	$880.00	pmn
20-Jul	ABBOTT	Ray's	$56.50	pmn
	J Anderson			
21-Jul	SHRR	Ray's	$84.00	pmn
	R Kraus			
	K Lespance			
21-Jul	DIXFIELD	Sullivan's	$350.00	pmn
	J Eder			
	D Levitsky			
22-Jul	NANOTECH	Piper's	$130.00	pmn
	M Nold			
	K Lister			
	J Porter			
22-Jul	PHOENIX	Ray's	$140.00	pmn
	M Moran			
		Roxy's Escorts	$750	
23-Jul	FURMAN	Red Snapper		
	J Lerner		$150.00	pmn
		Totals	**$2,579.00**	**$1,829.00**

Exhibit 7

NITA STATE FOOTBALL

YR-2 RECRUITING RATING—QUARTERBACK

NAME:	Fulbright, John ("Jackie")
POSITION:	Quarterback
HIGH SCHOOL:	Nita Central High School
Graduation:	YR-1
Academic Eligibility (ACT, SAT or Grade Point):	Established
INTEREST IN NITA STATE:	Low, will likely go to Penn State (father played there)
RATINGS:	
Foot Speed:	A+
Arm Strength:	A
Throw on Run	
Right:	A
Left:	B+
Size:	A- (6'2" 215 lbs)
Decision Making:	A+
Leadership:	A+
QUALITY OF HIGH SCHOOL COMPETITION:	B+
HIGH SCHOOL WIN/LOSS RECORD:	A
OPTION OFFENSE POTENTIAL:	A+
PRO-STYLE OFFENSE POTENTIAL:	A
OVERALL:	A

Exhibit 8

Photograph of John Fulbright Playing Football

Photograph of Helmet

Exhibit 10

Photograph of Entrance of Restaurant

Exhibit 11

Photograph Toward Clay

Exhibit 12

Photograph Toward Forest

Exhibit 13

M GO BLUE

March 12, YR-2

John Fulbright
2942 Rivington Road
Nita City, Nita 57819

Dear Jackie:

As one quarterback to another, I want to encourage you to consider the University of Michigan as the place to fulfill your football dreams. As I'm sure you know, unlike another team in our conference that I won't mention other than to say your dad played there, the Wolverines have sent a number of quarterbacks to the NFL in recent years, including me. This is where you want to be groomed for a pro career. It worked for me, and I'm sure it will work for you.

I know you have the potential for a great college and pro career if you get the right coaching in the right offensive scheme with quality opponents. Michigan offers all that plus a great educational opportunity as well. A full scholarship should be available as part of the package.

I would enjoy talking with you in person about your future plans. We have a bye the first week in November, and I'd love to come to Nita City to meet you and your folks. Just call me at home in Ann Arbor (743-555-8877) and let me know if we can get together.

Keep chucking,

Drew Cash

Drew Cash

Exhibit 14

LONGHORN FOOTBALL

UNIVERSITY OF TEXAS

AUSTIN, TEXAS

May 28, YR-2

Jackie Fulbright
2942 Rivington Road
Nita City, NITA 57819

Dear Jackie:

There's no place on this planet that loves its football more than the state of Texas. And there's no university that's more football crazy than UT. I'm writing because one of our graduates, Heisman Trophy winner Ricky Williams, just happened to be in the stands to see you lead your team to the Nita City championship. He called me right afterwards and couldn't stop talking about that last-minute drive where you coolly, calmly led your team down the field for the winning score. Ricky told me you already had a pro arm and were the man we needed to lead our team to another national championship.

When can we expect a visit from you, Jackie? UT has the finest facilities in the country for our football players. I would like to show you around campus, have you meet some of our players, and especially take you through our new football facility including our gourmet steakhouse, new weight training center, new locker room facility, and our new practice field. I'm sure you are in line for a full scholarship, and I'd also like to share with you all of the benefits of our nationally renowned summer work program.

Hook 'em Horns—

Campbell Earl

Campbell Earl
Backfield Coach

Exhibit 15

Penn State Nittany Lions
College Station, PA

April 6, YR-2

John Fulbright
2942 Rivington Road
Nita City, Nita 57819

Dear Jackie:

Our head football coach has asked me to write to tell you of our growing interest in your career, and our desire to see you in a Nittany Lion uniform after you graduate from high school. Everyone in the Penn State family of course knows of your father's exploits both here at College Station and in the NFL, and we are certain you care cut out to follow in his footsteps, only at quarterback rather than linebacker.

While we are best known for our defense, a look at the states will show we have sent many a quarterback into the NFL, myself included. As quarterback coach I would enjoy working with you to continue that tradition. I know you have the right stuff. And I can guarantee you there is no offensive line in the country that protects its quarterback better than ours at Penn State.

Let me know when you and your dad can come for a visit to talk about our program, scholarship availability, and your future here at Penn State. Coach and I look forward to seeing you both.

Sincerely,

MATT CAVANAUGH

Matt Cavanaugh
Quarterback Coach

Exhibit 16

University of Colorado Football
Boulder, Colorado
Home of the Buffs

March 15, YR-2

John Fulbright
2942 Rivington Road
Nita City, Nita 57819

Dear John:

I was recently given films of all your games this past season and I must say I am very impressed. You've got a great passing arm and surprising poise for a high school junior. I've talked with our coaches and I can assure you there will a quarterback slot wide open for you at CU should you sign with us. We have had freshmen start at quarterback here before with great success and with your skills, you would likely get four years of experience as a starter here, which is so valuable if you want to turn pro.

All of us associated with Buffalo football hope you will seriously consider CU as the place to play college Division One ball. If you come out to visit, I can assure you my colleagues and I in the Alumni Association will see to it you have the finest of times.

See ya soon,

Chuck Sisk

Chuck Sisk
President, Buffalo Football Alumni Assn.

Exhibit 17

Photograph of Motorcycle

Exhibit 18

Photograph of Parker's Car

Exhibit 19

Nita City
GENERAL HOSPITAL

Medical Records

I hereby certify that the attached 4 pages are true and accurate copies of the General Hospital medical records of patient John Fulbright for July 20, YR-2.

J.R. Yoowing

Assistant Medical Records Librarian

Exhibit 20

Nita City
GENERAL HOSPITAL

Emergency Department

PRESENTING COMPLAINT: Motor Vehicle Accident

ARRIVED BY: Ambulance | TIME: 15:05

CONDITION ON ADMISSION	FAIR	GOOD	COMA	HEMORRHAGE
	X			

ACCIDENTAL INJURY:	NO	YES	DATE:
		X	7/20/YR-2

John Fulbright
2942 Rivington Road
Nita City, Nita 57819

ALLERGIES	NO	YES	SPECIFY:

TIME:	TEMP.	PULSE	RESP.	B.P.	TIME:	TEMP.	PULSE	RESP.	B.P.
15:10	98.8	70	18	120/80	15:50	98.7	66	17	115/78

NURSE'S NOTES: Pt. reports loss of consciousness—
Unsure of duration. Moderate headache. Oriented x3

MEDICATIONS: N/A

NURSE'S SIGNATURE: K. Lansing

HISTORY AND PHYSICAL: **HY:** 17-y-o male in motorcycle
collision without helmet when Cadillac pulled into
right-of-way without signaling. Pt's speed at 20–25.
Complains of headache, pain R. extremities.
EXAM: Multiple minor contusions and abrasions,
chest sounds normal, abdomen nontender, neuro
exam negative.

DOCTOR'S ORDERS

	CBC		UA
	EKG	X	CHEST X-RAY
X	Skull x-ray		
X	R arm and leg x-ray		
X	Head CT		
	All X-rays normal		
	IMMUNIZATION		
	SUTURE NO.		

TREATMENT: Abrasions cleaned and dressed. Instructed parents to watch for signs of
post-concussive syndrome and to check every 3 hours overnight. Return p.r.n. or see

family doctor. Acetaminophen and ibuprofen p.r.n.

DIAGNOSIS: (1) Mild closed head injury | DIAGNOSIS CODE: S06.0X1A

(2) Multiple abrasions and contusions | S00-T14, T14.8

PHYSICIAN: I. Rodriguez, MD

DISCHARGED--CONDITION Good | TIME: 20:45 | ADMITTED—ROOM NO. | TIME:

PATIENT'S PHYSICIAN C. Barron, MD | ☐ CONTACTED AT _____AM/PM | ☐ UNABLE TO CONTACT | NOTIFIED RELATIVE MEDICAL EXAMINER

REFERRED TO | ☐ CONTACTED AT _____AM/PM | ☐ UNABLE TO CONTACT | POLICE BY: TIME:

INSTRUCTIONS TO: J. Fulbright and parents | DATE:

(PATIENT'S NAME) | (HOSPITAL #)

I understand I received emergency care only. I am to call the physician listed below for follow-up care.

Dr. C. Barron (Call for appointment)

I also acknowledge that I have received and understand the emergency physician's instructions.

Instructor's Signature ____________________ Patient's signature John Fulbright

Exhibit 21

Nita City
GENERAL HOSPITAL

MRI Report

I have been requested to provide a summary of an MRI which I ordered and interpreted for Mr. John Fulbright. I am Dr. Bridget Suparna and I am a board-certified radiologist practicing at General Hospital. I was contacted by the parents of John Fulbright in September YR-2 in regards to receiving an MRI. Both Jackie and his parents reported that he had been experiencing headaches, increased anger, and trouble with sustained attention recently. They noted he was involved in a motorcycle wreck on July 20, YR-2. I ordered an MRI to ensure he was not experiencing neurological injury that could potentially be life endangering.

He was given an MRI Brain without contrast. I would note this was his first MRI, and as such, no previous MRIs were available for comparison. His MRI showed no acute intracranial abnormalities. There was some evidence of potential mild gliosis in the right temporal lobe. Gliosis is scarring and can be caused by previous head injuries. Given the type and nature of his gliosis, I cannot conclude when the original injury occurred; however, the recent motorcycle accident is a possible cause and would explain the reported symptoms.

Sincerely,

Bridget Suparna

Bridget Suparna, MD

MRI BRAIN WITHOUT CONTRAST

Fulbright, John

Patient ID: 7831748

Final Result

MRI BRAIN W/O CONTRAST

History: Pt reported increased frustration and difficulty with concentration subsequent to MVA

Comparison: None available

Impression:

1. No acute intracranial abnormality. Some mild gliosis (scarring) visible in right temporal lobe.

Exhibit 22

Photograph of Martini

Exhibit 23

E-Serve Report
July 20, YR-2 Lunch

T:3	P:2
Chic Caesar	11.95
Marco Panini	9.95
Well Martini	8.00
Well Manhat	8.00
Coffee	3.00
Decaf	3.00
Pretax total	43.90
Tax	2.60
Total	46.50

T:16	P:2
Chic Caesar	11.95
Fish/Chips	9.95
House Chard	7.00
Bass Ale	5.50
Pastry Cart	5.00
Coffee	3.00
Coffee	3.00
Pretax total	45.40
Tax	2.72
Total	48.12

T:7	P:2
Chic Caesar	11.95
Pasta Special	10.95
KJ Chard	9.00
KJ Chard	9.00
Decaf	3.00
Coffee	3.00
Pretax total	46.90
Tax	2.81
Total	49.71

T:19	P:2
Steak Sand	14.95
Past Special	10.95
Prem Martini	10.00
Bud Light	5.00
Coffee	3.00
Tea	3.00
Pretax total	46.90
Tax	2.81
Total	49.71

T:12	P:2
Chic Caesar	11.95
Hamburger	9.95
F. Fries	3.00
D. Coke	3.00
Ice Tea	3.00
Pastry Cart	5.00
Pastry Cart	5.00
Coffee	3.00
Pretax	40.90
Tax	2.46
Total	43.36

T:24	P:2
Soup Special	5.00
Hamburger	9.95
Chic Panini	8.95
Well Martini	8.00
Well Martini	8.00
Ice Tea	3.00
Pretax total	42.90
Tax	2.57
Total	45.47

Exhibit 24

JOCKDATES.COM

Jackie

18 – Central City, Nita -- man

My self-summary

I'm a huge sports fan, a good student, and a really nice guy. I'm fit and athletic. I'm friendly, loyal and trustworthy.

What I'm doing with my life

In junior college, hoping to transfer to Penn State

I'm really good at

Athletics, school and working with people

Favorite books, movies, shows, music, and food

Harry Potter, Friday Night Lights, Breaking Bad, Country/rock, Pizza

The six things I could never do without

The NFL, the NCAA, the NBA, my family, my dog, girls. Not necessarily in that order.

I spend a lot of time thinking about

My former life as a quarterback and my future life as a coach.

On a typical Friday night I am

Out with friends.

You should message me if

You like someone who really likes sports.

New! Incognito Mode

I'm looking for

- Women
- Ages 18–20
- Near me
- Who are single
- For new friends, long-term dating

My details

Orientation	Straight
Ethnicity	White
Height	6' 2" (1.88m)
Body type	Athletic
Diet	Mostly anything
Smokes	No
Drinks	Socially
Drugs	Never
Religion	Christianity, and somewhat serious about it

Exhibit 25

Jamie Parker

From: Jamie Parker <jparker@americraft.nita>
Sent: July 20, YR-2 3:52 p.m.
To: Aaron Morrow <amorrow@americraft.nita>
Subject: RE: RE: My lousy day

The kid that hit me looked bad. I thought at first he might be dead. The car jockey at Ray's told me he was doing at least 50 when he hit me and flew off his bike.

Thanks, pal.

From: Aaron Morrow <amorrow@americraft.nita>
Sent: July 20, YR-2 3:50 p.m.
To: Jamie Parker <jparker@americraft.nita>
Subject: RE: My lousy day

Jamie – Under control. There's hardly anything a martini won't help. Anybody hurt?
Aaron

Aaron Morrow
Region 1 Sales Manager
Americraft Industries
4300 Industrial Highway
Central City, Nita

From: Jamie Parker <jparker@americraft.nita>
Sent: July 20, YR-2 3:45 p.m.
To: Aaron Morrow <amorrow@americraft.nita>
Subject: My lousy day

Aaron,

Missed my appointment with Ronnie Rivers. Had a long lunch with the purchasing asst from Abbott and then some punk on a motorcycle ran into me as I was leaving Ray's. Cops took forever. Please call Ronnie and smooth it over. I'm staying home for the rest of the day. Maybe I can call it a sick day from PTSD. Does a martini help PTSD?

Jamie

Jamie Parker
National Sales Manager
Americraft Industries
4300 Industrial Highway
Central City, Nita

Expert Materials

Expert Report of Morgan Myer, PhD (Plaintiff's Expert)

Myer Trauma Recovery
LLC

Morgan Myer, PhD

Re: Summary of Treatment and Evaluation for Mr. John Fulbright

Dear Plaintiff's Attorney,

My name is Morgan Myer, PhD. I am currently practicing as a licensed psychologist in Nita City. My practice, Myer Trauma Recovery LLC, has been open for the last twenty years. It is designed to provide therapeutic treatment to individuals who have experienced significant trauma. Trauma can have many forms—physical, mental, and emotional. The challenges of recovering from such traumas may also require both physical and emotional intervention and therapies. In my therapeutic treatment, I design individualized interventions based on the type of trauma and current difficulties in life.

I was referred to provide treatment for Mr. John Fulbright after his family indicated that he presented with some difficulties in functioning after being involved in a motorcycle accident where he was thrown from his motorcycle and sustained injuries. After being involved in the wreck, his family indicated that he had challenges with emotional regulation, maintaining attention, and completing tasks. They noted this was a marked change, because he had previously functioned exceptionally well in high school. He was a highly acclaimed football player, maintained adequate academic performance, and was socially active with both family and friends. I completed an evaluation and began treatment with Mr. Fulbright. I have been contacted and asked to summarize my findings and opinion on his current condition. I have not previously submitted my evaluation and treatment records for legal proceedings, so if additional information is necessary, please contact me. I was asked to include my fee per hour. As this is my first time working in a legal setting, I am billing at the rate of all my therapeutic and evaluative work, which is $250 per hour.

As the majority of my experience has been in working with individuals after trauma, I understand the vital importance of psychological assessments as a part of developing a treatment plan. I began by administering the Weschler Adult Intelligence Scale—Fourth Edition (WAIS-IV). The WAIS-IV is an individually administered clinical instrument designed to assess the cognitive ability of adults. The test provides subtest and composite scores that represent intellectual functioning in specific cognitive domains, as well as composite scores that represent general intellectual ability or Full Scale IQ. The test is organized into four composite indexes: Verbal Comprehension, Perceptual Reasoning, Working Memory, and Processing Speed. These four indexes are combined to produce the measure of Full Scale IQ. Descriptions of the individual indexes as well as Mr. Fulbright's scores and the interpretation of those scores are provided below.

The Verbal Comprehension Index (VCI) is a measure of the formation of verbal concepts, verbal reasoning, and a measure of knowledge acquired from the environment (typically school). Mr. Fulbright's score placed him in the 55th percentile as compared to same-aged peers. The Perceptual Reasoning Index (PRI) is a measure of nonverbal reasoning and decision making incorporating spatial processing and visual-motor integration. Mr. Fulbright scored within the 60th percentile as compared to same-aged peers. The Working Memory Index (WMI) provides a measure of working memory abilities. Working memory tasks require the ability to temporarily retain information in memory, perform some mental operation with the information, and then produce a result. Working memory involves attention, concentration, and reasoning. Mr. Fulbright's score placed him within the 6th percentile relative to his same-aged peers. The Processing Speed Index (PSI) provides a measure of ability to quickly and correctly scan, sequence, or discriminate simple visual information. This is not only a measure of speed, but also of decision-making and reasoning under time constraints. Mr. Fulbright's score placed him in the 5th percentile when compared to same-aged peers.

Mr. Fulbright put forth his best effort throughout all testing, despite periods of frustration or perceptions that he may have answered incorrectly, indicating that his scores are likely reflective of his best performance. His combined efforts generated a Full Scale IQ within the average range.

Per the report of himself and his family, his scores are not consistent with his general functioning over the course of his life. He reported that prior to the wreck, school had been "not fun, but easy enough." Although his grade point average was 2.4, he described that his GPA was not reflective of his best effort. He described in depth that he typically completed the minimum required in classes by choice, as he devoted the majority of his energy and effort to football. He stated that this was essential to his plan to become a professional football player, and was endorsed by his family and coaches.

I must acknowledge that because he did not experience prior academic difficulty, I do not have previous IQ testing to which I can compare his current scores. However, despite the lack of comparison, I would note that his scores are highly correlated with profiles of individuals with Traumatic Brain Injury (TBI)[1]. In short, his VCI and PRI scores are within the average range; however, his WMI and PSI scores show significant deficits. Again, this type of differentiation in subscales is reflective of TBI. While his overall intelligence is not likely reduced, he shows difficulty in memory and quick decision-making. These types of deficits are also related to other areas in which he described difficulty in functioning, such as frustration tolerance, emotional regulation, and sustained attention. I would note that these problems are particularly devastating for Mr. Fulbright, as they also would be the types of skills required to call and execute plays as a college and later professional football quarterback.

While Mr. Fulbright does have a long and illustrious history in football, he has not sustained previous serious injuries that could account for this TBI. He acknowledged that he had experienced hits that made him feel like he got his "bell rung"; however, such minor injuries would not typically accrue to the extent that they would cause the deficits with which he currently presents. Similarly, I must integrate the information obtained by his most recent MRI, which showed some evidence of scarring associated with TBI.

1. Biederman, J., Feinberg, L., Chan, J., et al. (2016), "Mild Traumatic Brain Injury and Attention Deficit Hyperactivity Disorder in Young Student Athletes," *Journal of Nervous and Mental Disease* 203(11), p. 813–819.

Diagnosis: **G31.84 Mild Neurocognitive Disorder due to traumatic brain injury with behavioral disturbance (mood disturbance and agitation)**

It is my opinion, based on available evidence, that Mr. Fulbright suffered a TBI injury as a result of the accident on July 20, YR-2. He currently experiences multiple symptoms associated with the TBI that impact all levels of his functioning. In addition, he will be unable to pursue any career in football. As a result of this trauma, he has sustained both physical and psychological injuries. After I completed my initial evaluation with him, I recommended that Mr. Fulbright begin treatment with me to address his trauma. We engaged in weekly therapy focused on recognizing and defining the effect of the trauma and designing appropriate treatment to increase his emotional coping, attention span, and grief over the loss of his potential career in professional sports. In my opinion, he has much to overcome as a result of this wreck. He would benefit from additional resources and therapy to help him redefine his future goals and heal from his current trauma.

Respectfully,

Morgan Myer

Morgan Myer, PhD

MORGAN MYER, PHD

Myer Trauma Recovery
LLC

Myer Trauma Recovery, LLC
2639 First Boulevard
Nita City, Nita 57817
(819) 555-4920

CURRENT LICENSURE

State of Nita License No. 185034

EXPERIENCE

Myer Trauma Recovery LLC, Owner and Lead Psychologist, YR-20 to present

As a psychologist who focuses in recovery from trauma, I begin with an assessment of all patients and then build an appropriate treatment plan to address all concerns and return the patient to maximum functioning.

Nita State Hospital, Staff Psychologist, YR-25 to YR-20

Staff psychologist working on inpatient trauma unit, treating complex trauma which required inpatient hospitalization. Both physical and emotional trauma were treated. Typically involved formal assessment to determine deficits in functioning.

Fellowship in Clinical Psychology, Arizona State University, YR-26 to YR-25

Full time commitment working at the college counseling center providing individual and group therapy, as well as assessment. I initiated a specialized therapy group for trauma survivors.

Internship in Clinical Psychology, University of North Carolina at Chapel Hill, YR-27 to YR-26

Full time APA accredited internship providing individual, group, and couples therapy to students attending the university. Also coordinated with treating psychiatrists.

EDUCATION

Doctor of Philosophy, Counseling Psychology, Pennsylvania State University, YR-30–YR-26

Master of Education in Counseling, University of South Carolina, YR-32–YR-30

Bachelor of Arts in English Literature, College of Charleston, YR-36–YR-32

AWARDS AND PUBLICATIONS

Awarded Psychologist of the Year, *Trauma Psychologists in Treatment Magazine*, YR-3

Awarded Exceptional Volunteer for Nita General Hospital, Trauma Center, YR-5

Myer, M. (YR-6), "Why Do I Feel This Way? Separating Physical and Emotional Symptoms After a Significant Trauma," *Getting Better Magazine*, 103–105

Penland, B. and Myer, M. (YR-15), "Fighting for the Little Guy: How Evaluation, Treatment, and Advocacy are Central to an Ethical Practice Treating Those with Complex Trauma," *Journal for Trauma Recovery* 29(4), 301–314

2

EXPERT REPORT OF LEE TIPPETT, MD (DEFENSE EXPERT)

LT

LEE TIPPETT, MD
BOARD CERTIFIED FORENSIC PSYCHIATRIST

To Whom It May Concern:

My name is Dr. Lee Tippett and I have been retained by the defense team with this case to provide a thorough examination of Mr. John Fulbright. I was retained at the rate of $500/hr. for consultation, evaluation, and writing and $700/hr. for testimony. I am currently a licensed psychiatrist and am board certified in both general and forensic psychiatry. My practice is limited to forensic evaluations in civil and criminal litigation. While I may make recommendations regarding treatment, I am not a treatment provider. I have not been in the role of treatment provider since completing my fellowship. I was asked to determine what, if any, diagnosis Mr. John Fulbright may have and to what extent it is related to the accident that occurred on July 20, 2022.

Sources of Data

1. Review of medical records from General Hospital
2. Statement given by John Fulbright
3. Review of medical records from Bridget Suparna, MD
4. Summary of Treatment and Evaluation for John Fulbright completed by Morgan Myer, PhD
5. Interview with John Fulbright

Informed Consent

Mr. Fulbright presented at my office for this evaluation. He was informed that I was retained by the defense, and no information would be considered confidential. He agreed to participate in the evaluation.

Relevant History

Mr. John Fulbright presented to this evaluation as a 19-year-old male. He reported he was raised by his mother and father. He denied any history of special education. He reported that he began to play football in childhood, in part because of his father's previous career as an NFL player. This incident occurred when he was 17 years old and enrolled in high school.

Mr. Fulbright's historical academic performance is also notable, in part, because his performance is minimally compliant with what is required. Within his statement he reported, "I wasn't the best of students in high school." I compared this to his current performance at Nita Community College, where his current GPA is 3.6.

The accident occurred on July 20, YR-2. Mr. Fulbright reported that since the accident he has struggled with some elements of attention and concentration. He also described extensive sadness associated with reports from medical professionals that he is not cleared to return to football, in part because of evidence of potential previous concussions. He also reported that he and his long-term girlfriend had ended their relationship, which he attributed to feelings of sadness associated with his post-accident recovery.

As Mr. Fulbright is still quite young, he has not yet established a career, obtained job training, married, or fathered children. As previously reported, he is currently attending Nita Community College.

Medical, Psychiatric, and Substance Use History

Mr. Fulbright reported no significant medical history. He said that prior to this accident he had never been admitted to the hospital, received surgical intervention, or experienced significant physical trauma. While his verbal self-report may be consistent with his experience, I must acknowledge that with a history of playing football since childhood, he did likely sustain repeated injuries. For example, within his statement he described having sustained injuries during football practices and games that required him to sit out and monitor himself for symptoms of concussion. In addition, he reported incidents of having his "bell rung," referring to immediate symptoms associated with forcible hits.

Mr. Fulbright denied any previous treatment or evaluation for mental health prior to the accident. There were no records provided that would indicate otherwise.

Mr. Fulbright denied any previous use of alcohol or drugs. He emphatically stated that he would never drink or use drugs, because it would negatively impact his performance in sports.

Current Functioning

Mr. Fulbright presented to the evaluation as a 19-year-old male. His physical presentation was above average. He appeared tall, fit, and well groomed. He was oriented to person, place, time, and situation. His speech was normal with regard to rate, volume, and tone. His thought process was logical, coherent, and complex. Based on his performance within this evaluation, I would estimate his intelligence to be within the average to high average range.

When asked about his current functioning, he reported difficulty with attention and concentration. He also described extended feelings of grief and despondence associated with not being able to play football. Despite these feelings, he appears to function exceptionally well within his life. He attends college full time, has promising plans for the future, and maintains social relationships with his friends and family.

Review of Records

General Hospital Medical Records: Mr. Fulbright was brought by ambulance to the emergency department of General Hospital on the date of the accident. He was examined for injuries. He was found to have various lacerations and contusions. He described having a headache. He was ordered to receive a series of X-rays, which showed no fractures. An MRI was not requested or required at that time, as no overt evidence of neurological injury was noted.

Review of MRI by Dr. Bridget Suparna: An MRI was requested by Mr. Fulbright's family approximately six weeks after the accident. They reported that he appeared to have difficulty with emotional regulation, lowered frustration tolerance, and some difficulty with completing tasks. Dr. Suparna reviewed the available imaging and determined that although there were some possible areas of small scarring in the temporal lobe, the MRI was largely normal. It should be noted that even with the documentation of possible scarring, the cause of such scarring cannot be determined, because the MRI could not be compared to previous MRIs, as this was his first.

Summary of Treatment and Evaluation for John Fulbright completed by Morgan Myer, PhD: Mr. Fulbright was seen by Dr. Myer after having been referred for mental health treatment regarding difficulty coping. Dr. Myer administered the Weschler Adult Intelligence Scale—Fourth Edition, an IQ test, to determine his level of functioning. His full scale IQ was within the normal range. His performance showed deficits with regard to working memory and processing speed. Dr. Myer opined that such deficits were due to traumatic brain injury (TBI), which Dr. Myer believed was sustained on July 20, YR-2. Dr. Myer listed a diagnosis of mild neurocognitive injury due to traumatic brain injury with behavioral disturbance.

Conceptualization

In reviewing all available documents, I integrated information from Mr. Fulbright's verbal self-report as well as collateral data obtained through prior medical examinations and psychological testing. To briefly summarize, Mr. Fulbright asserts that after the accident in YR-2, he began to experience symptoms that he believed were caused by the accident. This included increased frustration, decreased attention, and general difficulty in coping. While Dr. Myer attributed these changes in functioning to a possible traumatic brain injury (TBI), I believe Dr. Myer did not fully consider other relevant information. First, those reviewing this information should note that Mr. Fulbright participated in football beginning in childhood. Those individuals who consistently play football are at increased risk of repeated injuries, including concussions. Secondly, it cannot immediately be concluded that deficits in his WAIS-IV scores are associated with the injuries sustained during the accident. Frankly, his subscale scores are consistent with individuals with attention deficit hyperactivity disorder (ADHD). Those individuals with ADHD often present with difficulty in attention and processing speed although they maintain average IQ overall. Finally, an evaluator must acknowledge the ways in which emotional difficulty associated with grief may impact testing. Mr. Fulbright is a young man whose dreams of playing in the NFL will not come to fruition. This, in and of itself, may account for increased frustration, decreased coping, and problems with attention. While all people who meet with Mr. Fulbright may understand that he is a young man struggling with a future he did not anticipate, none of these challenges can conclusively be connected to the accident.

Diagnosis

F43.25 Adjustment disorder with mixed disturbance of emotions and conduct.

Conclusions

Mr. Fulbright is a young male who reported that since the accident on July 20, YR-2, he has experienced multiple neurological symptoms, which previous evaluations associated with possible TBI. A thorough examination of the information, including a review of a recent MRI, showed no definitive TBI. Current testing is reflective of potentially previously undiagnosed ADHD as well as grief associated with alterations in his future plans. I would recommend that Mr. Fulbright continue with therapeutic intervention to increase his coping skills; however, it is my opinion that none of his current symptoms are caused by or the direct product of the accident. As an alternative, I would encourage him to focus on his current increased GPA and academic success at his current community college.

If you have any additional questions, I can be contacted by email or phone.

Sincerely,

Lee Tippett

Lee Tippett, MD

CV of Lee Tippett, M.D.

LT

LEE TIPPETT, MD

BOARD CERTIFIED FORENSIC PSYCHIATRIST

LICENSURE

State of Nita,
Medical License No. 009921

STATEMENT

I am a board certified forensic psychiatrist who has practiced solely in the area of forensic assessment for the past 10 years.

EXPERIENCE

FORENSIC PSYCHIATRIST • TIPPETT MEDICAL CLINIC • YR-11–PRESENT
My practice is exclusively devoted to forensic assessment in civil and criminal litigation. I conduct evaluations and assessments of clients involved in legal cases, summarize my findings, and provide written reports to retaining parties. As a part of conducting an evaluation, I am always available to testify as needed.

FELLOWSHIP IN FORENSIC PSYCHIATRY • UNIVERSITY OF CINCINNATI • YR-12–YR-11
Full-time training dedicated to providing forensic evaluations for diverse populations served by the University of Cincinnati and affiliated organizations and hospitals. Conducted for both criminal (competency to stand trial, mental state at the time of the offense, competency to waive *Miranda*) as well as civil (custody evaluations in divorce proceedings and civil liability/damages).

RESIDENCY IN PSYCHIATRY • UNIVERSITY OF CINCINNATI • YR-16–YR-12
Four-year standard residency training involving practice in all areas of psychiatry. Chief Resident as PGY-4.

EDUCATION

MEDICAL DEGREE • YR-16 • NORTHWESTERN MEDICAL SCHOOL
Summa Cum Laude

BACHELOR OF SCIENCE • YR-19 • UNIVERSITY OF CENTRAL FLORIDA
Summa Cum Laude, Captain of Debate Team

EMAIL | TWITTER HANDLE | TELEPHONE | LINKEDIN URL

LT

LEE TIPPETT, MD

BOARD CERTIFIED FORENSIC PSYCHIATRIST

PUBLICATIONS AND SPEAKING ENGAGEMENTS

"Who's an Expert? Working to Educate the Judicial System on Restricting Forensic Evaluations to Those who are Truly Qualified," *Psychiatric Practice*, September YR-6

"Practice Makes Perfect: How to Refine Your Practice so it Fulfills Your Income Goals," Nita State Psychiatric Association Yearly Conference YR-9

"TBI, ADHD, and Bipolar Disorder: How Cultural Preoccupation Leads to Overdiagnosis and Damages our Profession," *Psychiatric Ethics* YR-11

EMAIL

TWITTER HANDLE

TELEPHONE

LINKEDIN URL

www.ingramcontent.com/pod-product-compliance
Lightning Source LLC
LaVergne TN
LVHW082352200926
848481LV00012B/3548